The Food Cost

Mastery

Fusion of Academic Rigor and Industry Expertise

Wissam Baghdadi

RESTAURATOMY

"This book is lovingly dedicated to my late parents, whose encouragement and belief in my abilities led me to the world of hotel management when I was just thirteen. They saw potential in me long before I saw it in myself, guiding me towards a path filled with passion and purpose. Their inspiration has been a constant source of strength and motivation throughout my career, and every page of this book carries a piece of the wisdom and love they instilled in me. It is in their memory that I strive to excel and share the knowledge they helped me discover.

"To my family, whose unwavering love and support have been my greatest treasures. You are my driving force, my safe haven, and my greatest inspiration. A special dedication goes to my children, who fill my life with joy, purpose, and endless motivation. You are the reason I strive to achieve more every day, and I hope this book inspires you to follow your dreams with the same passion and determination. This is for you.

Contents

Preface

A Journey into Hospitality and Beyond

In 1991, during one of the last phases of the Lebanese Civil War, I found myself captivated by stories of faraway places and adventures that seemed almost mythical. My late father often spoke about Hotel Management, describing it as a noble profession filled with opportunities for travel and discovery. He would recount his travels across Europe in the 1960s, where he journeyed by car from Beirut, exploring cities, cultures, and the landscapes of a continent still healing from its past. Each story, each adventure, painted a picture in my mind of a life filled with excitement, new experiences, and endless possibilities.

One day, I asked him what a hotel manager does. He paused, a thoughtful smile crossing his face, and replied, "A hotel manager pays attention to every little detail and ensures that high-quality service is delivered to every guest." Those words ignited a spark in me. I loved the idea of being meticulous, of crafting an experience for others down to the finest details. It seemed a perfect marriage of my interests—a career that could fulfill my love of travel and my passion for hospitality.

By 1995, I had begun to seriously consider a career in hotel management. After some research, I contacted L'École Hôtelière de Lausanne in Switzerland, spurred on by advice from my father's cousin who lived there. The school welcomed me with an offer to sit for an assessment test. It was a dream, but one that quickly faded when I realized the tuition was far beyond what I could afford.

Undeterred, I began exploring other paths. In 1996, driven by my fascination with travel, I even considered becoming a pilot. I dreamed of soaring through the skies, visiting new places, and experiencing that sense of adventure I had always imagined. I would lay awake at night, hearing the distant hum of airplanes overhead, imagining the cozy world of passengers tucked into their warm seats, suspended between worlds at 3:00 a.m. But the reality set in—at $400 an hour, flight school was also out of reach.

In 1997, a different opportunity presented itself. My cousin decided to take an English course at the British Council, and I decided to join him. I realized that improving my English could open doors to universities worldwide, including those offering programs in hospitality. Over two years, I honed my English skills, eventually passing the Cambridge Proficient Exam for English Speaking and Listening.

Then, in 1998, a serendipitous conversation in the schoolyard changed everything. A friend mentioned he was heading to Australia to study hotel management, where he could work and study simultaneously to cover his tuition fees. It was a eureka moment for me—the perfect solution that aligned with my dreams and financial situation. Just three months later, I was on a plane to Sydney, Australia, embarking on my very first journey out of Lebanon. It was also my first time on an airplane, an experience that took me through several layovers: Beirut, Larnaca, Dubai, Singapore, Melbourne, and finally, Sydney. The Thirty-six-hour trip was long and uncomfortable, but every moment felt like a step closer to my destiny.

From the moment I landed in Australia, I dove headfirst into my new life. During my first week at the Blue Mountains International Hotel Management School (BMIHMS), I approached the Industry Placement office, eager to start working. When asked what skills I had, I laughed and admitted, "Nothing yet, but I'm willing to do whatever it takes, even clean toilets."

The officer smiled, "With that attitude, you'll go far in this industry."

My first job was as a dishwasher at Felton Woods Manor in Katoomba, NSW. It was a humble beginning, but I embraced it wholeheartedly. Working closely with the family that ran the manor, I learned the basics of hospitality—from preparing pâté and crusted bread to garnishing plates between dish cycles. I remember vividly the first time the chef, with his thick Aussie accent, asked me to fetch parsley from the cold room. I stood there for ten minutes in the freezing cold, clueless about what he had asked for, until he kindly showed me each ingredient.

The first year was a whirlwind of new experiences—learning, adapting, and growing. I was noticed by one of my professors for my hospitality skills, and one day, he pulled me aside and offered me a job at a new restaurant he was opening in Sydney. Without hesitation, I said yes. The restaurant, Baia San Marco, located in Cockle Bay Wharf, was a fast-paced environment where I learned the ins and outs of running food and interacting with customers despite my limited English skills. I still laugh when I remember the two gentlemen on Australia Day who simply wanted a couple of beers, but I thought they had a complaint.

By 2002, I had graduated with a BA in International Hospitality & Tourism from BMIHMS and Bournemouth University. I moved to Dubai, a city buzzing with growth and opportunity, and found myself with multiple offers within the hospitality industry. Surprisingly, I chose a different path—joining Emirates Airlines as a flight attendant. It was a nod to my childhood dream of flying, and for three adventurous years, I traveled the world, always scoring top marks in my assessments and fast-tracking to become a Senior Flight Steward.

Yet, my heart yearned for something different, something closer to my original passion. So, I decided to start my own restaurant with a close friend in Algiers, Algeria. The restaurant, A La Grande, was my first true test—a one-man show from concept to completion. I was the designer, builder, manager, and chef. Without an architect, I hired a mason, electrician, plumber, and carpenter, piecing together my vision step by step. I slept on the restaurant tables, cleaned at 1:00 a.m., and woke up at 6:00 a.m. to prepare for breakfast. It was grueling, but it was mine. Through it all, Amira, who would later become my wife, stood by my side. Despite her own demanding job as a flight attendant with Emirates, she supported me endlessly, bringing back a piece of art from every city she traveled to. These vintage posters from the '60s, '70s, and '80s decorated the walls, adding soul and character to the diner-style concept we were building together. Her belief in my vision and her thoughtful touches made A La Grande more than just a restaurant, turning it into a space that reflected both of our journeys.

One unforgettable night during the 2006 World Cup, we had a full house, and all orders came in at once. The kitchen was a flurry of activity when suddenly, our grill, under intense heat, warped and mixed all the proteins together. In that split second, I had to decide: apologize to the customers and start over, close the kitchen, or keep going. I chose the latter. After a moment of hysterical laughter with my team, we continued. The guests, engrossed in the Brazil vs. France game, barely noticed. Moments like these deepened my passion for this industry.

Returning to Dubai in 2006, I joined Al Tayer Group as a Country Manager, later transitioning to Business Development for their F&B division. I revitalized a struggling flagship store, slashing food costs from 36% to 24% and boosting monthly revenue fivefold. I opened new branches, sourced suppliers, dealt with municipal approvals, and fine-tuned the art of menu engineering. I began importing and developing international franchises, gaining invaluable experience that would serve me well in future endeavors.

By 2009, I was freelancing, taking on challenges like launching Fauchon in Dubai Mall and advising a chocolate company in Abu Dhabi. Then, in a twist of fate, I joined Del Monte, a company where I would spend over a decade growing businesses, developing concepts, and spearheading innovative projects. I built a multimillion-dollar café concept from scratch, opening a total of forty-five branches across various locations. Some evolved, some closed, and new ones took their place, continually adapting to the market. I also led the launch of the world's first Pink Pineapple in North America, turning it into a viral sensation.

As my journey with Del Monte came to an end in 2022, I found myself at a crossroads, ready to embrace new opportunities. I founded Restauratomy, a boutique consultancy for restaurants, and partnered with a tech company Jalebi.io to create a revolutionary restaurant operating system. In 2023, I took on the role of COO at Caffeine Lab, a forward-thinking coffee company that has allowed me to further expand my strategic expertise in the food and beverage industry. I realized there was a gap in the industry— a lack of comprehensive knowledge connecting all the dots. So, I began writing, pouring my experiences into what would become "The Food Cost Mastery."

And here I am, sharing this story with you, dear reader. It's been over twenty-seven years in the making, a journey filled with ups and downs, challenges, and triumphs. I hope this book serves as a valuable resource, drawing from all I have learned and experienced, and inspires you in your own journey through the fascinating world of hospitality.

Introduction

Welcome to "The Food Cost Mastery," a guide born from years of hands-on experience in the restaurant and food service industry. This book is not just a compilation of strategies and principles; it's a reflection of the lessons I've learned over decades of working in various facets of the food business. From my early days as a student at the Blue Mountains International Hotel Management School (BMIHMS) to my role as COO of a leading coffee company, I've navigated the complexities of food cost management across different types of establishments—whether it's a high-end fine dining restaurant, a casual dining concept, or a fast-paced quick-service restaurant (QSR).

What is Food Cost Management?

Food cost management has always been at the heart of my professional journey. It's more than just crunching numbers; it's about understanding the intricate balance between quality, customer satisfaction, and profitability. I remember the first time I truly grasped the importance of food cost management during my time at BMIHMS. We were tasked with running the Bistro, and with limited resources, we had to feed 265 students over a weekend. It was there that I learned the significance of every decision—from sourcing ingredients to portion control—each one directly impacting our ability to stay within budget while delivering a quality product.

Why is Food Cost Management Important?

Throughout my career, I've seen firsthand how effective food cost management can make or break a restaurant. Whether you're dealing with the rising costs of ingredients or managing a team of chefs and kitchen staff, understanding and controlling food costs is crucial. It's not just about survival in this competitive industry; it's about thriving. "The Food Cost Mastery" delves into these complexities, offering you the same strategic insights that have helped me optimize operations and drive profitability in every role I've held.

What Can We Learn From The Food Cost Mastery?

This book covers everything you need to know about food cost management, from the basics to advanced strategies. Drawing from real-world examples and personal experiences, I've included the critical topics that have shaped my approach to running successful food businesses:

- **Financial Planning and Budgeting:** My approach for financial planning and budgeting is to set achievable financial goals and meticulously plan budgets, ensuring sustainable profitability.

- **Food Cost Percentage:** Here, I'll explain how I've used food cost percentages to scrutinize and optimize menu pricing in various settings, from upscale restaurants to casual eateries.

- **Average Check and Sales Mix:** Techniques I've honed through years of experience I have come to understand how variations in the sales mix affect the average check and how leveraging capitation ratios can be a game-changer in predictive planning and maximizing profitability.

- **Discounts and Promotions:** I will share all the insights I've gained from years of managing discounts and promotions effectively, understanding their impact on food costs, and integrating them into financial strategies without eroding margins.

- **Inventory Management and Movement:** This will conclude all the advanced techniques I've developed over the years for tracking inventory efficiently, minimizing waste, and optimizing stock levels.

- **Yield Management:** By using real-life examples of how I maximized ingredient usage, like using vegetable peels for stocks during my early days in the kitchen, we will understand yield management.

- **Demand-Based Pricing:** Strategies I've developed for adapting pricing based on market trends and consumer behavior, helping to maximize profitability through responsive pricing techniques, will get us through the concept of demand-based pricing.

- **Competitive Analysis:** I will share all the methodologies that I've refined for conducting competitive analyses that and inform strategic pricing and positioning, ensuring a competitive edge in the market.

- **Inventory Turnover:** This part includes the techniques I've utilized to manage and optimize inventory turnover, including practical approaches to visualizing product expiry and ensuring efficient stock rotation.

- **Managerial Techniques:** I've compiled every single insight into the key managerial techniques that I've employed over my career, including effective negotiation with suppliers and the critical roles of purchasing and procurement.

- **Tax Considerations:** The guidance I've provided on managing tax implications within financial reporting, ensuring that food cost calculations are accurate and reflect true net operational costs, will pave the way and make you an expert in dealing with taxes.

Tools and Techniques

Throughout this book, I've included practical examples, step-by-step formulas, and illustrative tools that have been instrumental in my success. These are not just theoretical concepts but tried-and-tested methods that have helped me navigate the challenges of the food service industry.

Advanced Topics

We will also explore cutting-edge topics that are shaping the future of food cost management. From integrating restaurant operating systems (ROS) to utilizing artificial intelligence for enhanced decision-making, this book will give you the tools to stay ahead of the curve in a rapidly evolving industry.

Conclusion

Whether you're starting a new venture or looking to refine your existing operations, "The Food Cost Mastery" is designed to be your essential resource. By the end of this book, you'll be equipped with the knowledge and strategies to meticulously control your food costs, optimize your operations, and significantly enhance your profitability.

These are the insights that have guided me through my career, and I'm excited to share them with you.

This expanded introduction aims to encapsulate the scope, depth, and practical value of "The Food Cost Mastery," setting the stage for a transformative learning experience.

Part One:

Introduction to Food Costing

What is Food Costing?

We have already provided a brief overview of what Food Costing is. Now we can go into detail and explain everything about it so you will have no questions left in your mind.

From my own experience, food costing has been the cornerstone of every successful operation I've managed. I recall a time early in my career when a simple miscalculation in food costs led to shrinking profit margins without us realizing it. It was only through rigorous food costing that we were able to identify the issue and make the necessary adjustments, which not only stabilized our finances but also gave us the confidence to price our menu items more competitively. Food costing isn't just about numbers — it's about ensuring that every decision you make is grounded, giving you the control needed to run a profitable business.

Why Food Costing Matters?

Food costing is crucial in the restaurant and catering industry as it directly impacts profitability. Understanding food costs helps in setting the right prices for menu items, ensuring that each dish contributes adequately to covering costs and generating profit. It also aids in financial planning, allowing businesses to forecast expenses and revenues accurately. By maintaining control over food costs, businesses can prevent financial losses and improve their overall financial health.

These points highlight the commonly accepted reasons why food cost management is essential. However, based on my extensive experience and the insights shared throughout this book, I believe there are additional layers to consider:

1. **Strategic Resource Utilization:** Food costing is not just about controlling expenses but about maximizing the use of every ingredient in the kitchen. By understanding and implementing effective costing strategies, you can optimize

inventory usage, reduce waste, and ensure that every item contributes to the bottom line. This approach is particularly critical when managing multiple outlets or a central kitchen where resource allocation can significantly impact overall profitability.

2. **Empowering Decision-Making:** Accurate food costing provides the data-driven insights necessary for making informed strategic decisions. Whether it's about adjusting menu prices, negotiating with suppliers, or launching a new product line, food costing serves as the backbone of operational and financial planning, enabling you to adapt swiftly to market changes while maintaining profitability.

3. **Capturing Inventory Movements:** Effective food costing requires a meticulous approach to tracking every movement of inventory, from receiving and storage to preparation and final sale. Capturing these movements accurately is essential for maintaining inventory integrity, reducing discrepancies, and ensuring that all costs are accounted for in the financial analysis.

These additional perspectives underscore the importance of a holistic approach to food costing—one that goes beyond just numbers and integrates strategic thinking into the fabric of restaurant management.

Key Terms and Concepts

To navigate the complexities of food costing effectively, every hospitality professional should be familiar with the following key terms and concepts:

Key terms in food costing include:

Food Cost Percentage:

Food cost percentage is a critical metric in the restaurant and catering industry. It represents the ratio of the cost of ingredients to the revenue generated from a dish. This percentage helps evaluate whether menu prices are set appropriately and if the business is maintaining a healthy profit margin.

Formula:

$$\text{Food Cost Percentage} = \frac{\text{Cost of Ingredients}}{\text{Revenue from Dish}} \times 100$$

Example:

Let's learn food cost percentages with some very common examples. Suppose a restaurant sells a Seafood Pasta dish for $20. The cost of ingredients for this dish is $5.

$$\text{Food Cost Percentage} = \frac{\$5}{\$20} \times 100 = 25\%$$

This means that 25% of the revenue from the pasta dish goes towards the cost of ingredients. To maintain a healthy profit margin, the restaurant must ensure that the food cost percentage aligns with its financial goals, typically aiming for a percentage between 20% and 25% as the cost of ingredients alone.

In my experience, understanding and controlling the food cost percentage has always been more than just about the numbers—it's about making informed decisions that can make or break a business. When I first started working in the industry, I quickly realized how crucial this metric is. At one of the cafes I managed, where beverage sales accounted for a significant portion of revenue, we kept our beverage costs low, which helped balance the overall food cost percentage. This allowed us to allocate more of our budget to premium ingredients for our food menu without sacrificing profitability. This experience taught me the importance of tailoring cost strategies to fit the specific dynamics of each business.

This food cost percentage varies between businesses. A coffee shop, for instance, relies on the sales of beverages that typically have a lower cost percentage, such as coffee, tea, and other base ingredients. Whereas restaurants that serve food typically have a higher cost percentage.

Gross Margin:

Gross margin is the difference between revenue and the cost of goods sold. It indicates the profitability of individual menu items.

Formula:

Sales – Cost of Goods Sold (COGS) = Gross Margin (GM)

$$\frac{\text{Gross Margin}}{\text{Sales}} \times 100 = \text{Gross Margin Percentage}$$

Example:

Suppose the restaurant's monthly sales are $100,000 and the cost of goods sold is $25,000.

$100,000 (Sales) – $25,000 (COGS) = $75,000 (GM)

$$\text{Gross Margin\%} = \frac{\$75,000}{\$100,000} \times 100 = 75\%$$

This means that 75% of the revenue is available to cover all overheads and achieve the desired parameter of Net Profit.

We once implemented a seasonal menu featuring premium ingredients that increased our COGS temporarily. By carefully monitoring our gross margin, we were able to adjust our pricing strategy accordingly, ensuring that our profitability remained strong despite the higher ingredient costs. This experience underscored the importance of regularly analyzing gross margins to maintain a healthy balance between cost and revenue.

General Cost Components in the Restaurant Industry

Understanding and managing the various cost components in a restaurant is key to maintaining profitability and ensuring the sustainability of the business. Throughout my career, I've encountered and managed these costs in various capacities, from running my own restaurant to overseeing operations in large-scale enterprises. Let's break down these costs into categories and discuss how they impact your business.

Fixed Costs

Fixed costs are the backbone of your restaurant's budget, as they remain consistent regardless of your sales volume. During my time managing multiple outlets, the predictability of fixed costs allowed us to better plan our financial strategies, even during off-peak seasons. These are costs you can count on, such as:

- **Rent:** A non-negotiable monthly expense that must be met regardless of how many guests walk through the door.
- **Salaries:** For salaried employees, these costs remain the same every month, making it easier to plan your budget.
- **Insurance:** Essential for protecting the business from unforeseen events.
- **Utilities:** While some utilities can fluctuate, basic services like water and sewage are generally consistent.

Understanding fixed costs is crucial, as they form the foundation of your budget. In my experience, it's these predictable expenses that often give you the breathing room to innovate in other areas.

Variable Costs

Variable costs, unlike fixed costs, fluctuate based on your restaurant's activity. I recall periods of high customer volume where our ingredient costs soared, requiring careful management to maintain profitability. These costs include:

- **Cost of ingredients**: A direct reflection of what's on the menu and how much is sold.
- **Packaging**: This is especially relevant in today's delivery-focused market, where the cost can vary widely.
- **Utilities**: Electricity and gas usage often spike during busy times, impacting your variable costs.

Effectively managing variable costs is where true cost control lies. By reducing waste, negotiating better supplier contracts, and optimizing processes, you can significantly impact your bottom line. I've seen firsthand how these strategies can turn a struggling restaurant into a profitable one.

Direct Costs

Direct costs are the heart of food costing—they are the costs directly tied to the production of your menu items. Accurate tracking here is non-negotiable. During my career, ensuring precise cost allocation to each dish was crucial for maintaining healthy profit margins. These costs include:

- **Raw materials and ingredients**: The actual food items used in your recipes.

I've always emphasized the importance of transparency and accuracy in managing direct costs. Without it, you risk mispricing your menu and losing profitability.

Indirect Costs

Indirect costs, or overheads, are just as critical, though they don't directly tie into the production of food. In various roles, I've seen how these costs can quickly add up if not managed properly. These include:

- **Administrative expenses**: These keep the back-end operations running smoothly.
- **Marketing and advertising costs**: Essential for driving customer traffic but must be carefully balanced against the return on investment.
- **Maintenance and repairs**: A well-maintained kitchen ensures smooth operations, and neglecting this can lead to unexpected costs.

- **Labor or Payroll:** These are often the most significant expenses after food costs. While it's challenging to allocate these costs directly to specific dishes, they are essential for the overall operation. I've always believed in training and retaining quality staff because, in the long run, a skilled workforce saves money through efficiency and better customer service.

In my experience, indirect costs can be the silent killers of profitability if not carefully monitored. For instance, in a previous role, I noticed that marketing spending wasn't yielding the expected returns, leading us to shift our strategy for better results.

In summary, managing these cost components effectively requires a detailed understanding of where every dollar is going. Over the years, I've seen that a successful restaurant operation hinges on a delicate balance between controlling costs and delivering quality. By understanding and monitoring these costs, you can set your business up for sustained profitability.

Calculating Food Costs

Accurately calculating food costs is the backbone of effective restaurant management. It's not just about tracking expenses—it's about understanding every element that contributes to the cost of each dish on your menu. Over the years, I've learned that calculating food costs is not just about numbers; it's about understanding the entire ecosystem of your kitchen. I remember during my time at BMIHMS, we had to run the Bistro over a weekend, tasked with feeding 265 students on a limited budget. There was no profit involved—just the challenge of stretching our funds to ensure everyone was well-fed. This experience taught me that even the smallest detail mattered—from how much olive oil was used per dish to the cost of garnishes. This meticulous attention to detail allowed us to manage our resources effectively and ensured that we could meet our goal within the given budget. It's these experiences that have ingrained in me the importance of being thorough and precise in food cost management.

In this section, we'll delve into various strategies for calculating food costs, from recipe costing to yield management. These techniques may seem distinct, but they are all interconnected, contributing to the overall accuracy of your food cost calculations. By mastering these methods, you can refine your pricing strategies, control expenses, and ultimately enhance your profitability.

Let's look at these various techniques.

What is Recipe Costing?

Recipe costing is the process of calculating the total cost of all ingredients used in a dish. This foundational practice involves meticulously measuring each ingredient, determining its cost based on the purchase price, and summing these to establish the total cost per serving.

I vividly remember my first class at BMIHMS, Restaurant Catering Management (RCM), taught by one of our Chef Professors. It was during this class that something just clicked for me—a light bulb moment where I realized that I was born to understand this or born to do this, as it came to me naturally. The process of breaking down recipes, calculating the cost of each dish, and understanding the financial impact of every ingredient fascinated me. This passion has stayed with me throughout my career, driving my commitment to precision and efficiency in recipe costing.

Accurate recipe costing is the foundation of setting menu prices that cover costs and generate profit.

Let's take a look at:

Sample Recipe Card

Recipe Name: Classic Margherita Pizza

Recipe Type: Main Course

Portion Size: One Pizza

Recipe Card:

Ingredients	Qty	UOM	Qty	UOM	Cost per Unit	Total Cost
Pizza Dough	0.25	kg	0.55	lbs	$ 6.00	$ 1.50
Pizza Sauce	0.125	l	4.23	fl oz	$ 3.20	$ 0.40
Mozzarella	0.125	kg	0.28	lbs	$ 10.20	$ 1.27
Basil Leaves	0.5	g	0.02	oz	$ 0.80	$ 0.40
Olive Oil	0.015	l	0.51	fl oz	$ 20.00	$ 0.30
Salt	0.5	g	0.02	oz	$ 0.02	$ 0.01
					Total Cost	$ 3.97
					Selling Price	$15
					Food Cost %	26.46

This approach allowed me to create detailed recipe cards for every dish on the menu, enabling me to closely monitor and control recipe costs.

What is Portion Control?

Portion control is the process of dividing ingredients into specific amounts to ensure consistency in serving sizes and to control costs. It is an essential step for maintaining consistency in serving sizes, which directly affects both cost control and customer satisfaction. By standardizing portions, you can minimize waste and maintain consistent cost per dish, which is integral to achieving accurate food costing.

I owe my understanding of proper portioning to one of my friends, who was already a chef before joining BMIHMS as a student. Back in the year 2001, our group was assigned to operate all kitchens at BMIHMS for an entire week—an especially significant week as it marked the ten-year foundation day of the school. The experience was intense and unforgettable. I still vividly remember the detailed Excel sheets we used to track and manage portion sizes for every dish. It was during this time that I truly learned the importance of precision in portioning, a lesson that has stayed with me throughout my career.

In the context of the Margherita Pizza recipe, portioning ensures that each pizza has the same amount of dough, sauce, cheese, and toppings, resulting in consistent quality and cost control.

Standardizing portions reduces waste and ensures that the cost per dish remains consistent, aiding in accurate food costing.

Suggested Example of Portioning in the Margherita Pizza Recipe:

- **Pizza Dough:** One ball of pizza dough is portioned for one pizza. Each portion weighs approximately 0.250 kg (250 grams) or 0.55 lbs.
- **Tomato Sauce:** Half a cup of 125 ml or 4.23 fl oz. of tomato sauce is used per pizza.
- **Fresh Mozzarella:** 0.125 kg (125 grams) or 0.28 lbs. of mozzarella are portioned for each pizza.
- **Fresh Basil Leaves:** 0.5 grams or 0.02 oz. per pizza.
- **Olive Oil:** 0.15 l (15 ml) or 1 tbsp. per pizza.
- **Salt:** 0.5 grams or 0.02 oz. per pizza.

By pre-portioning these ingredients, the kitchen staff can quickly assemble pizzas with minimal waste and ensure each pizza tastes the same.

What is a Batch Recipe?

Batch recipes are preparations of large quantities of a particular ingredient or dish that can be portioned out for individual servings.

Batch recipes facilitate the preparation of large quantities of a component used across various dishes. This method enhances kitchen efficiency and ensures consistency in taste and cost. It is especially useful for commonly used ingredients or menu items.

My first encounter with the importance of batch recipes was while operating a chocolate concept in Abu Dhabi. We had a particularly popular hot chocolate drink that flew off the shelves during rush hours. To keep up with demand and prolong the shelf life, we started preparing batches of semi-finished chocolate without adding the cream, which was only mixed in later, closer to the serving time. This method allowed us to chill the cocoa mix and have it ready in large quantities. These batches were a game-changer, enabling us to serve customers quickly and consistently, even during the busiest times. This experience taught me the critical role batch recipes play in maintaining operational flow and meeting customer expectations in high-demand situations.

Example of Batch Recipes Used in the Margherita Pizza Recipe:

Pizza Dough:

- **Batch Recipe:** A large batch of pizza dough can be prepared in advance and divided into individual balls for portioning.
- **Suggested Ingredients for Batch:**
  - Flour: 2 kg or 4.41 lbs.
  - Water: 1.2 liters or 40.58 fl oz.
  - Yeast: 20 grams or 0.71 oz.
  - Salt: 40 grams or 1.41 oz.
  - Olive Oil: 50 ml or 1.69 fl oz.
- **Suggested Procedure:** Mix all ingredients, knead until smooth, let rise, and then divide into 0.250 kg (250 grams) or 0.55 lbs. balls.
- **Suggested Yield:** Approximately twelve portions/balls of dough.

Tomato Sauce:

- **Batch Recipe:** A large batch of tomato sauce can be prepared and stored for use in multiple pizzas.
- **Suggested Ingredients for Batch:**
  - Canned Tomatoes: 4 kg or 8.82 lbs.
  - Olive Oil: 0.2 l (200 ml) or 6.76 fl oz.
  - Garlic: 20 grams or 0.71 oz. (minced)
  - Basil: 50 grams or 1.76 oz. (chopped)

- Salt: 20 grams or 0.71 oz.
  - **Suggested Procedure:** Sauté garlic in olive oil, add tomatoes and basil, simmer until thickened, and season with salt.
  - **Suggested Yield:** Approximately 7.5 liters or 7.93 quarts of sauce, 30 portions, 250 ml or 8.45 fl oz. (0.26 qts) per portion.

By preparing these batch recipes, the kitchen can efficiently produce large quantities of dough and sauce, which can then be portioned for individual pizzas as needed. This reduces preparation time during service and ensures consistency in the final product.

What is The Yield Concept?

Yield tests measure the amount of usable product after processing. For example, the yield of vegetables after peeling and chopping.

Understanding the yield—measurable as the usable product after processing—is crucial for accurate recipe costing.

This is a critical aspect of kitchen management, helping to determine the actual usable amount of an ingredient after processing and to accurately cost recipes.

Here are some subsections that would offer you examples of common ingredients, showing the original and usable weights and explaining how this affects costing.

Understanding Yield Percentage

- **Usable Weight:** The weight of the ingredient after processing (e.g., peeling, trimming, cooking, etc.)
- **Original Weight:** The weight of the ingredient before processing.

Example Calculations

- **Oranges for Orange Juice**
  - **Original Weight:** 10 kg or 22.05 lbs. of whole oranges.
  - **Suggested Usable Weight:** 5 kg or 11.02 lbs. of orange juice after peeling and juicing.

Note: This means that 50% of the original weight of oranges is lost during juicing.

Weight could be converted to volume to form a cup of orange juice.

- **Salmon from Whole to Fillet**
  - **Original Weight:** 2 kg or 4.41 lbs. of whole salmon.
  - **Suggested Usable Weight:** 1.4 kg or 3.09 lbs. of fillet after removing skin, bones, and head.

Note: This means that 30% of the original weight of salmon is lost during filleting.

Example Yield Calculation Table

Below is a sample of the suggested yield calculation table for different ingredients:

Ingredient	Original Weight	Original Weight	Usable Weight	Usable Weight	Yield Percentage
Oranges	10 kg	22.05 lbs.	5 kg	11.02 lbs.	50%
Whole Salmon	2 kg	4.41 lbs.	1.4 kg	3.09 lbs.	70%
Potatoes	5 kg	11.02 lbs.	4 kg	8.82 lbs.	80%
Carrots	3 kg	6.61 lbs.	2.4 kg	5.29 lbs.	80%
Chicken (whole)	1.5 kg	3.31 lbs.	1.1 kg	2.43 lbs.	73%

Reducing waste not only lowers costs but also supports sustainability. This part shows you how you could utilize kitchen remnants effectively, transforming potential waste into valuable kitchen resources.

- **Vegetable Peels, Stalks, and Ends:** Use to make flavorful vegetable stock.
- **Meat and Poultry Bones:** Create rich stocks and broths.
- **Stale Bread:** Transform into breadcrumbs or croutons.
- **Fruit Scraps:** Make flavored syrups, kinds of vinegar, or jams.
- **Herb Stems:** Add to stocks, sauces, or use as aromatics.
- **Cheese Rinds:** Enhance soups and sauces with extra depth of flavor.

By implementing these strategies, you can maximize the use of all ingredients, reduce waste, and improve the overall efficiency of your kitchen.

In my first year at BMIHMS, I was assigned to the Production Kitchen (PK), where I had one of my earliest experiences with yield management. I remember vividly how the Chef instructed me to save all vegetable peels, ends, and scraps—things I would normally discard at home. These remnants were tossed into an enormous tilt pan, simmered in water overnight, and by the next morning, we had a rich vegetable stock. This stock was then frozen in portions and used in other dishes throughout the week. That experience not only taught me the value of every part of the ingredient but also how effective yield management could contribute to both sustainability and cost efficiency in the kitchen.

Packaging Costs in Restaurant Operations

Packaging plays a critical role in the food service industry, directly influencing costs and operational efficiency. The choice between including packaging costs in recipes or treating them as consumable items varies across businesses, but understanding these costs is essential for accurate financial planning. This section explores the implications of different packaging strategies and offers insights into managing these costs effectively.

Necessary vs. Additional Packaging

Packaging can be categorized into two types: necessary and additional.

Necessary packaging is essential for serving the product and typically includes items like paper wraps or cardboard boxes for burgers, which are sufficient for dine-in scenarios.

Additional packaging, such as carry bags, is required for takeaway orders and represents an extra cost that needs to be managed separately.

Direct Recipe Integration Method

For precise cost management, many restaurants differentiate their recipes based on dine-in (DI) and take-away (TA) scenarios. A dine-in recipe might not factor in the cost of packaging, while a take-away recipe will include it to reflect the true cost of service. This method ensures that inventory depletion is accurately recorded based on the customer's choice at the point of sale. When orders are placed, the service staff confirms whether the order is for dine-in or take-away, and the POS system adjusts inventory and cost calculations accordingly. Having two recipes, one for DI and one for TA, is the direct integration method.

Modified Order Method

Restaurants can also manage packaging costs through a modified order strategy where each packaging material is treated as a separate recipe component. For example, if a customer orders a meal for dine-in, the base recipe without packaging is used. If the order changes to take-away, additional items like carry bags are added as modifiers, allowing for precise tracking and depletion of packaging materials from the inventory.

Both methods are particularly useful in quick-service restaurants (QSRs) and coffee shops, where the DI and TA are extensive and equally popular.

In my experience, managing packaging costs has always been a crucial aspect of maintaining profitability, especially in fast-paced environments like QSRs and coffee shops. I vividly recall a time in KSA when I introduced a new system in one of the chains I managed. We had been struggling with accurately tracking packaging costs, particularly with the surge in takeaway orders. I implemented a modified order method, where every packaging material—whether a cup, lid or carry bag—was treated as a separate component in the recipe. This approach not only allowed us to have precise inventory depletion but also provided clearer insights into where our costs were going. It was a game-changer in streamlining our operations and keeping our financials in check. Understanding these nuances can make all the difference in maintaining control over your restaurant's expenses and ensuring long-term success.

Inventory Turnover

Inventory turnover measures how quickly inventory is used and replenished. A high turnover rate indicates efficient inventory management, while a low rate may suggest overstocking or slow-moving items. Regular monitoring helps in optimizing stock levels and reducing holding costs.

Product Shelf-Life Explanation:

Day 1:

- **Product A1** (Batch 1) arrives with an expiry date of Day 10.

- **Product B1** (Batch 1) arrives with an expiry date of Day 15.

Day 5:

- **Product A2** (Batch 2) arrives with an expiry date of Day 20.

- **Product B2** (Batch 2) arrives with an expiry date of Day 25.

Day 10:

- **Product A1** is used first to avoid expiry.

- **Product A2** is still in stock, next in line for use.

Day 15:

- **Product B1** is used first to avoid expiry.

- **Product B2** is still in stock, next in line for use.

Timeline Diagram:

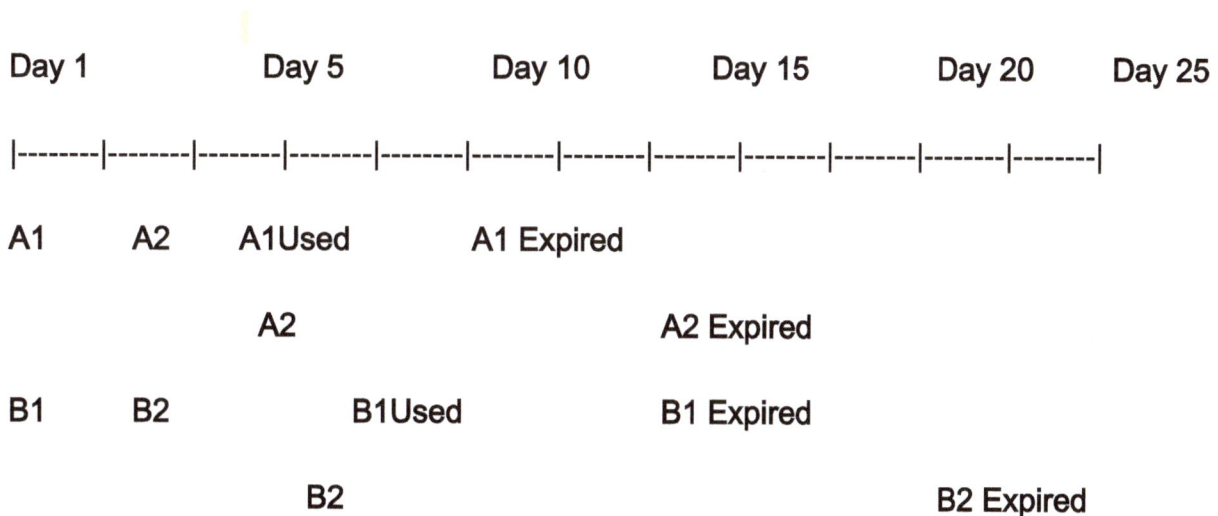

| Day 1 | Day 5 | Day 10 | Day 15 | Day 20 | Day 25 |

|--------|--------|--------|--------|--------|--------|--------|--------|--------|--------|--------|--------|--------|

A1   A2   A1Used   A1 Expired

                  A2   A2 Expired

B1   B2   B1Used   B1 Expired

                  B2   B2 Expired

"This timeline diagram illustrates the importance of proper inventory rotation and tracking to ensure products are used efficiently and wastage is minimized."

- **A1, B1**: Batch 1 of Product A and B (Arrives on Day 1, A1 expires on Day 10, B1 expires on Day 15).

- **A2, B2**: Batch 2 of Product A and B (Arrives on Day 5, A2 expires on Day 20, B2 expires on Day 25).

- **Used**: Indicates when the batch is used to avoid expiry.

- **Expired**: Indicates when the batch expires if not used in time.

Inventory Turnover and Product Expiry Timeline

Effective inventory management ensures that products are used in a timely manner, minimizing waste and maintaining product quality. The following timeline demonstrates how products should be rotated based on their expiry dates using the FIFO (First In, First Out) method:

Day 1:

- Product A1 is received and has an expiry date of Day 10.

- Product B1 is received and has an expiry date of Day 15.

Day 5:

- Product A2 is received and has an expiry date of Day 20.

- Product B2 is received and has an expiry date of Day 25.

Day 10:

- **Product A1** should be used first to avoid expiration, followed by **Product A2**.

Day 15:

- **Product B1 (Batch 1)** should be used first to avoid expiration, followed by **Product B2 (Batch 2)**.

First In First Out Practice (FIFO)

By adhering to the FIFO method, restaurants can ensure they use products in the order they were received, preventing older stock from expiring and reducing waste. This approach is essential for maintaining the freshness of ingredients and the overall quality of dishes served to customers.

Reducing Waste

Throughout my career, I've seen firsthand how waste can significantly impact a restaurant's bottom line. Early on, I realized that waste wasn't just about throwing away excess food—it was about lost opportunities for revenue. In my own restaurant in the city of Algiers, we noticed a troubling amount of food going to waste each week. It wasn't until we introduced stricter portion control and started implementing FIFO that we saw a dramatic reduction in our costs. But beyond the financial savings, it was the shift in mindset among the team that made the biggest difference. We started seeing ingredients as valuable resources rather than disposable items. This change in perspective not only improved our profitability but also fostered a more sustainable and responsible kitchen culture. Reducing waste is about more than just cutting costs—it's about maximizing what you have and creating a more efficient, sustainable operation.

Reducing waste involves implementing practices like:

FIFO (First In, First Out): Ensure older stock is used first.

Utilizing Whole Ingredients: Find creative ways to use every part of an ingredient.

Monitoring Expiration Dates: Implement a system for labeling and dating all stored items to ensure they are used within their optimal timeframe.

Proper Handling and Storage: Using airtight containers and proper refrigeration methods to extend the life of perishable goods

Portion Control: Use tools like scales and scoops to measure exact serving sizes, ensuring consistency and reducing excess use.

Inventory Management: Use inventory management software to track usage trends and prevent over-ordering.

Staff Training: Regular training sessions on proper cutting techniques, portion control, and efficient use of ingredients.

Creative Repurposing: Develop recipes that repurpose leftovers creatively. For instance, turning unsold fish into fish cakes or chowder.

Batch Cooking: Cook large batches of sauces, grains, or proteins that can be portioned out and used in various dishes to ensure all prepared food is utilized.

Donation Programs: Establish relationships with local charities to regularly donate excess food before it spoils.

Composting: Set up a composting system for organic waste and use the compost for the restaurant's garden where applicable.

Lean Production: Implement just-in-time cooking methods, where food is prepared based on actual customer orders rather than predictions.

Part Two:
Managerial Techniques

Managerial Techniques

Before delving into the specific strategies that address cost-saving and operational efficiency, it is crucial for you to establish a clear understanding of managerial techniques and their pivotal role in the restaurant industry. Managerial techniques are the cornerstone of effective restaurant management, enabling businesses to optimize their operations, reduce waste, and enhance profitability.

These techniques encompass a broad spectrum of practices, from refining kitchen workflows to adopting advanced inventory management systems and implementing energy-efficient practices. Each technique not only contributes to direct cost savings but also fosters a culture of continuous improvement and innovation.

In my years of running and optimizing restaurant operations, I've come to realize that managerial techniques are not just a set of practices—they are the backbone of successful restaurant management. These techniques have been instrumental in every establishment I've led, from casual dining to high-end restaurants. They've allowed me to navigate challenges, streamline operations, and drive profitability, often under less-than-ideal circumstances. Implementing these techniques has been a learning journey, one where I had to adapt, innovate, and sometimes rethink traditional approaches to fit the unique needs of each restaurant.

Why Managerial Techniques Matter

Adopting robust managerial techniques is fundamental for any restaurant aiming to thrive in a competitive market. They provide you with the framework for making informed decisions, streamlining processes, and ensuring that every aspect of the operation contributes positively to the bottom line. Effective management practices lead to:

- **Reduced Operational Costs:** By improving efficiency and reducing waste, you can lower your overall expenditure.

- **Enhanced Customer Satisfaction:** Streamlined operations ensure consistent quality and service, directly impacting customer satisfaction and repeat business.

- **Sustainability:** Implementing eco-friendly practices and reducing waste contributes to a restaurant's sustainability efforts, appealing to environmentally conscious consumers.

As we explore the various dimensions of managerial techniques in the subsequent chapters, from financial management to inventory control and beyond, keep in mind that these strategies are interlinked. Each technique not only addresses specific challenges but also complements others, creating a comprehensive approach to cost control and operational excellence. This section will equip you with the necessary tools and insights to implement these techniques effectively, ensuring your restaurant not only survives but also thrives in today's dynamic culinary landscape.

Implementing cost-saving strategies can significantly influence the bottom line. This includes optimizing kitchen operations to reduce waste, implementing energy-saving measures, and sourcing ingredients more cost-effectively. Continuous improvement in operations can lead to sustained cost savings.

Menu Engineering

Definition: Menu engineering is the study of the profitability and popularity of menu items and their strategic placement on a menu to maximize profits.

Introduction: One of my first experiences with menu engineering was with a franchise from Belgium. We had an extensive menu, but not all dishes were profitable or popular. It was like trying to sell air coolers in the Arctic. By categorizing items into "Stars," "Plow Horses," "Puzzles," and "Dogs," we were able to identify the dishes that were draining resources and those that were driving profits. This analysis allowed us to redesign the menu, focus on promoting the stars, introducing more stars, and ultimately increase our average ticket size and overall profitability. I still use this technique to this day. However, with today's advanced system reports, the job is much easier.

Application: Analyze the popularity and profitability of each menu item and categorize them into four groups: Stars (high profit, high popularity), Puzzles (high profit, low popularity), Plow Horses (low profit, high popularity), and Dogs (low profit, low popularity). Focus on promoting Stars, enhancing the appeal of Puzzles, adjusting pricing or ingredients for Plow Horses, and considering the removal or redesign of Dogs.

Standardized Recipes

Definition: Standardized recipes are detailed, written instructions used to prepare a dish so that it is consistently delivered to the customer with the same quality and portion size every time it is made.

Introduction: Standardizing recipes was a game-changer in one of the chains I managed. Before implementing standardized recipes, we had frequent complaints about inconsistencies in portion sizes and taste, especially across different branches. After rigorous uniformed training and ensuring that every dish was prepared using the same recipe, we saw a significant drop in customer complaints and an increase in repeat business. This consistency not only improved customer satisfaction but also helped in maintaining accurate food costs. Collecting feedback from customers is as good as the action taken afterwards, or the follow thru.

Application: Ensure that every dish is prepared using a standardized recipe to control portion sizes and ingredient usage. Train staff to follow these recipes precisely and regularly review and adjust the recipes to reflect ingredient cost changes or other operational updates.

Portion Control

Definition: Portion control involves managing the amount of food served to ensure consistent serving sizes, which helps in managing food costs and reducing waste.

Introduction: I remember a time when we struggled with fluctuating food costs at a busy Café. We discovered that the root cause was inconsistent portion sizes. By introducing portion control tools like scales and scoops and training the staff on their proper use, we were able to stabilize our food costs. This change not only reduced waste but also ensured that every customer received the same amount of food, leading to more consistent customer satisfaction.

Application: Use tools such as scales, scoops, and pre-portioned packaging to ensure consistent serving sizes. Implement portion control training for kitchen staff and regularly monitor adherence to these guidelines.

Waste Management

Definition: Waste management in a restaurant involves practices aimed at reducing the amount of waste generated and responsibly disposing of or reusing waste products.

Introduction: Waste management became a priority for me after a particularly eye-opening experience at my own restaurant. We were losing a significant amount of money due to over-preparation and spoilage. By implementing waste tracking systems and regularly conducting waste audits, we identified the key areas where we were losing money and took corrective actions. This not only saved costs but also aligned the restaurant with more sustainable practices, which resonated well with our customers.

Application: Track and analyze waste to identify areas where reduction is possible, such as over-preparation or spoilage. Implement composting, recycling programs and conduct regular waste audits to determine the causes of waste and implement corrective measures.

Inventory Management

Definition: Inventory management is the process of organizing and controlling stock levels to ensure adequate supplies without excessive surplus.

Introduction: Poor inventory management can quickly spiral into chaos, as I learned early in my career. In one restaurant where I waited tables, we frequently ran out of key ingredients and had too much stock going to waste. Implementing an inventory management system that tracked stock levels in real-time and setting up regular inventory counts transformed our operations. This system allowed us to maintain optimal stock levels, reduce waste, and avoid the last-minute panic of running out of crucial ingredients.

Application: Use inventory management software to monitor stock levels and usage patterns, helping prevent over-ordering and spoilage. Regular inventory counts should be compared with usage reports to identify discrepancies and prevent theft or loss.

Supplier Negotiations

Definition: Supplier negotiations involve strategic discussions with suppliers to secure the best prices, terms, and quality for products and services.

Introduction: Effective supplier negotiations have been a cornerstone of managing food costs in every restaurant I've run. I remember negotiating a significant discount on bulk purchases of high-quality produce by building strong relationships with multiple suppliers. This not only reduced our ingredient costs but also ensured a reliable supply chain. Good supplier relationships have always been about more than just price—they're about trust, reliability, and mutual benefit.

Application: Negotiate for better prices, bulk discounts, or favorable payment terms. Build strong relationships with multiple suppliers to encourage competition and secure the best deals.

Forecasting and Demand Planning

Definition: Forecasting and demand planning are processes of predicting future sales based on historical data and market trends to adjust business operations accordingly.

Introduction: Forecasting is an art as much as it is a science. During a peak season at an airport location during my time in KSA, accurate forecasting allowed us to plan our staffing and inventory needs precisely, avoiding both shortages and surpluses. This planning was crucial in maintaining service quality during the busiest times and helped us maximize profits when demand was at its highest. To be clear on this exceptional case, our sales were tenfold the regular busiest day.

Application: Use historical sales data to forecast future demand. Develop sales forecasts for different times of the year and adjust purchasing and staffing to match expected demand.

Labor Cost Management

Definition: Labor cost management involves strategies to optimize staff scheduling and productivity to align with business levels, ensuring cost efficiency.

Introduction: Managing labor costs has always been a delicate balancing act. In one of the cafes I managed, we initially struggled with overstaffing during slow periods and understaffing during rush hours. By analyzing sales patterns and using labor management software, we were able to create more efficient schedules. This adjustment not only reduced labor costs but also improved staff morale and service quality by ensuring we had the right number of staff at the right times.

Application: Schedule staff based on anticipated business levels to avoid overstaffing or understaffing. Use labor management software to create efficient schedules and monitor labor costs as a percentage of sales.

Energy and Utility Management

Definition: Energy and utility management in restaurants involves optimizing energy usage to reduce costs while maintaining operational efficiency.

Application: Implement energy-saving practices such as using energy-efficient appliances and turning off equipment when not in use. Regularly track utility usage and costs and invest in training staff on energy conservation methods.

Technology and Automation

Definition: Technology and automation refer to the use of advanced systems and software to streamline restaurant operations, reduce errors, and enhance efficiency.

Introduction: Technology has always been a key driver of efficiency in the restaurants I've managed. When we introduced a new Restaurant Operating System (ROS) at one of the chains, it revolutionized our operations. The system integrated inventory management, sales tracking, and customer preferences, reducing manual errors and freeing up time for staff to focus on delivering exceptional service.

Application: Use ROS systems to track sales, manage inventory, and analyze customer preferences. Invest in technology that integrates various aspects of restaurant management to reduce manual errors and improve operational efficiency.

Periodical Financial Analysis

Definition: Periodical financial analysis involves regular reviews of financial statements to evaluate a restaurant's financial health and identify areas needing improvement.

Application: Conduct monthly P&L reviews to analyze revenue, costs, and profitability. Use financial reports to make informed decisions about menu pricing, labor management, and other cost-saving measures.

Regular financial reviews have been critical to the success of every restaurant I've run. Monthly P&L reviews allowed us to spot trends, identify areas of concern, and make data-driven decisions to improve profitability. In one case, these reviews helped us identify a drop in sales during specific periods, leading to targeted promotions that successfully boosted revenue.

Training and Development

Definition: Training and development entail providing staff with ongoing education and training to enhance their skills, ensure compliance with industry standards, and improve service quality.

Introduction: Investing in staff training has always paid dividends. At one of the concepts that I created and led in the MENA region, we introduced a comprehensive training program focused on operations, food handling, portion control, and customer service. The impact was immediate—customer satisfaction scores improved, and we saw a reduction in food waste. Continuous training ensured that our team stayed sharp and adhered to best practices, which directly contributed to the restaurant's success.

Application: Regularly train staff on best practices for food handling, portion control, and customer service. Conduct refresher courses to ensure staff adherence to cost-control practices and service excellence.

Budgeting

Definition: Budgeting in a restaurant context involves planning financial targets for revenue and expenses to guide operations and financial decisions.

Introduction: Budgeting has always been a fundamental part of my approach to restaurant management. At a café chain I co-lead, setting realistic financial targets helped us navigate the uncertainties. Regularly reviewing our performance against these targets allowed us to stay on track and make necessary adjustments to our spending and pricing strategies.

Application: Set financial targets and regularly review actual performance against these budgeted figures to identify deviations and areas for improvement.

Monitoring and Analyzing Costs

Definition: Monitoring and analyzing costs involve regular examination of expenditure to track financial performance and identify opportunities for cost reduction.

Introduction: Cost monitoring has often been the difference between a profitable month and a loss. In one restaurant, we implemented a system to closely track food and labor costs, comparing them to sales daily. This vigilance allowed us to make quick adjustments, such as altering portion sizes or revising staff schedules, which helped keep our costs in line and maintain profitability.

Application: Regularly monitor and analyze costs to spot trends and variances. Review financial statements and track KPIs to conduct cost-benefit analyses, enabling early detection of cost overruns and timely corrective actions.

Part Three:

Inventory Management

Inventory Management

Introduction

Inventory management has always been one of the cornerstones of my approach to restaurant operations. Over the years, I've come to understand that it's not just about keeping track of what's in your storeroom—it's about ensuring that every item serves its purpose efficiently and contributes to the restaurant's bottom line. From my earliest days in the industry, I've seen firsthand how well-managed inventory can make or break a business. It's about having the right products at the right time, minimizing waste, and ensuring that every dish served meets the highest standards. This section delves into the strategies I've developed and refined throughout my career to help you achieve the same level of control and precision in your inventory management.

Description

Proper inventory management is a dynamic and comprehensive process that goes far beyond just storage. It's about developing a keen awareness of stock levels, usage patterns, and future needs. This awareness allows you to maintain a smooth operation, ensuring that your kitchen never runs out of key ingredients and that waste is minimized. In my experience, implementing robust inventory systems is critical not only for day-to-day efficiency but also for long-term financial health. These systems enable your restaurant to quickly adapt to changes in customer demand, seasonal ingredient availability, and fluctuations in supplier deliveries. By mastering inventory management, you can enhance your restaurant's resilience, reduce costs, and consistently deliver a high-quality dining experience.

Handling Measurements

Definition: Handling measurements in a restaurant involves accurately defining and using units of measurement for various ingredients and materials, which is essential for precise recipe formulation and inventory management.

Introduction: Effective measurement handling is foundational to accurate inventory management and cost control. This section explores the different units of measurement critical to a restaurant's operations, ensuring precision across purchasing, storing, and cooking processes.

Units of Measurement

Definition: In the restaurant world, units of measurement encompass volume, mass, bundles, and piece counts—each playing a crucial role in food preparation and inventory control. These units are the foundation upon which accurate recipes and efficient inventory management are built.

Introduction: From my early days in the kitchen, I quickly learned that precision is key, and that starts with understanding units of measurement. I remember one of my first kitchen jobs where a simple miscalculation—a mix-up between ounces and grams—threw off an entire batch of a signature dish. It was a hard lesson, but one that ingrained in me the importance of consistency in measurements. Applying the correct units across recipes, inventory records, and purchasing documents isn't just about numbers; it's about ensuring the quality and consistency of every dish that leaves the kitchen.

Techniques:
- Define the units of measurements between:
  - Volume *(fluids)*
  - Mass *(weight)*
  - Bundles *(like herbs)*

    and

  - Each or Piece *(i.e., ready-to-drink beverages, ready-to-eat food)*

- Consistency is Key:

  Use the same units of measurement throughout your operations—from recipes to inventory records to purchasing documents. This consistency is something I've always emphasized in the teams I've led. For example, if you purchase flour in large bags, store it in kilograms and use it in recipes measured in grams. This not only prevents conversion errors but also streamlines your inventory system. Feeding the conversion rates into your Inventory Management System ensures that everyone is on the same page, making operations smoother and more efficient.

Layers in the Units of Measurements Within Your ROS

Definition: Layers in measurement units refer to the various forms in which ingredients are bought, stored, and used, each requiring specific measurement units for accurate tracking.

Introduction: Proper training and system support are crucial for managing the layers of measurement units used in recipes, storage, and purchasing, enhancing consistency, and reducing errors.

Techniques:
- Step one is to choose an IMS/ROS that supports such a function.
- Train staff on the different units of measurement used in recipes, storage, and purchasing.
- Provide conversion charts and use digital scales and measuring tools that support multiple units to avoid discrepancies.
- Implement standard operating procedures (SOPs) for measurements.

Purchase Unit Vs. Storage Unit Vs. Recipe Unit

Definition: Layers in measurement units refer to the different forms in which ingredients are purchased, stored, and used—each requiring precise measurement units for accurate tracking and inventory management.

Introduction: My first real encounter with the complexities of layers in units of measurement came when I was tasked with adjusting the entire inventory for a

Belgian franchise I was running. At the time, I was using Fidelio Material Control as our IMS, and the ability to manage multiple layers in units of measurement was a game-changer. We discovered significant errors in unit conversions that were inflating our monthly food cost. By accurately defining these layers, we managed to drop the theoretical food cost from a staggering 36% to an actual 24%—a remarkable achievement that underscored the importance of precision in this area.

Techniques:

- **Step One:** Choose an IMS/ROS that supports multi-layered units of measurement. This capability is essential for accurate inventory management and cost control.

- **Staff Training:** Ensure that all staff members are trained on the different units of measurement used in recipes, storage, and purchasing. Proper training is critical for maintaining consistency and avoiding costly errors.

- **Tools and Conversion Charts:** Provide conversion charts and use digital scales and measuring tools that support multiple units. These tools help prevent discrepancies and ensure accuracy across all layers of measurement.

- **Standard Operating Procedure:** Implement SOPs for measurements to standardize processes and minimize the risk of errors. Consistent application of these procedures will lead to more reliable inventory tracking and cost management.

Conversion Rates of Units of Measurements

Definition: Conversion rates between different units of measurement are essential for accurately adapting ingredient quantities from purchasing to recipe execution, ensuring consistency and precision.

Introduction: My journey into mastering conversion rates began when I first realized how even a small miscalculation could snowball into significant discrepancies across inventory and recipe costing. I vividly remember an instance where a simple error in converting kilograms to grams led to inconsistencies in a batch recipe, which not only threw off our inventory but also affected the consistency of the dishes served. This experience taught me the importance of being meticulous with conversion rates and ensuring that the entire team was well-versed in these calculations.

Techniques:

- **Utilize conversion tools and software:** Employ reliable conversion tools and software to automate and ensure accuracy in measurement conversions. This minimizes the risk of human error and maintains consistency across the board.

- **Staff Training and Resources:** Provide comprehensive training and accessible resources like conversion tables for staff to reference. Ensuring that everyone follows the same standards is key to maintaining consistency and precision in both recipe preparation and inventory control.

Gross Weight Vs. Net Weight Vs. Strained Weight

Definition: Gross weight, net weight, and strained weight are critical measurements that reflect the weight of ingredients before and after preparation, essential for accurate costing and inventory tracking.

Introduction: In managing food costs, I've seen firsthand how even minor adjustments can significantly impact the bottom line. One instance that stands out is when we realized that our cost for Kalamata olives—a key ingredient in several of our popular dishes like Greek salad, olive bread, and tapenade—was consistently higher than the theoretical calculations. The discrepancy arose because we were calculating costs based on the net weight, not the strained weight, neglecting the fact that the water in which the olives were packed was discarded. Once we adjusted our costing to reflect the strained weight, we saw a noticeable improvement in our food cost accuracy, highlighting the importance of these distinctions.

Techniques:

- **Staff Training:** Ensure kitchen staff are trained to accurately differentiate between gross, net, and strained weights. This precision is crucial for calculating ingredient costs correctly, especially in items like canned goods where liquid is discarded.

- **Standard Operating Procedure:** Implement SOPs for weighing ingredients at different stages of preparation. For instance, always weigh items like olives after draining to ensure accurate cost calculations that reflect the true usable quantity.

Applying Yield Management

Definition: Applying yield management in measurements involves adjusting ingredient quantities in recipes to account for the actual usable portion after processing.

Introduction: Yield management involves determining the usable amount of an ingredient post-preparation, which is essential for precise costing and waste reduction. During my time working with Fidelio Material Control (FMC), I personally implemented the yield into recipes using the percentage method. The key was understanding that each dish's unique preparation could affect the yield differently, requiring careful calculation to ensure accuracy. By incorporating these yield percentages directly into recipes, I could better control costs and reduce waste across the kitchen.

Techniques:

- **Conduct yield tests regularly** determine the actual usable portion of ingredients after processing, such as peeling, trimming, or cooking. This helps establish a clear understanding of the conversion from gross weight to net weight, which is crucial for accurate measurement and costing.

- **Yield Documentation and Integration:** Document the yield percentages and integrate them into your measurement practices. For instance, if you purchase 10 kg (22.05 lbs) of potatoes and, after peeling, you are left with 8 kg (17.64 lbs) of usable product, calculate the yield percentage and apply this when determining the quantities required for recipes.

- **Measurements Adjustments:** Use yield-adjusted measurements in your recipes. For example, if a recipe requires 1 kg of peeled potatoes, you must account for the yield and start with more than 1 kg of unpeeled potatoes based on the yield percentage. This ensures the final measurement used in the dish is accurate.

- **Conversion Consistency:** Ensure that the yield percentage is consistently applied when converting between different units of measurement, whether moving from bulk purchase quantities to individual portion sizes or converting between metric and imperial units. This consistency ensures that every recipe accurately reflects the true cost and quantity of ingredients needed.

- **Recipe Calibration:** Regularly calibrate your recipes by adjusting ingredient quantities based on yield data. This practice ensures that your recipes remain accurate over time, even as ingredient sizes, suppliers, or preparation methods change.

Categorizing Inventory

Definition: Product categorization in inventory management helps organize stock in a manner that enhances tracking and utilization.

Introduction: Efficient categorization of products in inventory management facilitates streamlined operations and improved cost control by ensuring that items are accurately tracked and managed. Throughout my career, I've seen various approaches to categorizing inventory, each with its strengths and potential pitfalls. For example, I've worked with professionals who prefer to allocate milk separately for beverages and food production, segregating bar and kitchen inventory. However, I've found that creating multiple product entries for the same ingredient can lead to confusion, particularly when it comes to recipe management. Instead, I advocate for a simpler approach: using storage and requisition segregation. This method allows for clear tracking without complicating the inventory system, ensuring that an ingredient remains an ingredient, no matter where it's used in the operation.

Avoiding Duplicate Ingredients on a System

Definition: Preventing duplicates in inventory systems avoids confusion and errors in stock levels, ensuring accurate data for purchasing and usage.

Introduction: Minimizing duplicates in inventory entries is crucial for maintaining an organized and accurate stock system, helping to ensure that all inventory data is up-to-date and reliable. Throughout my career and even in my current role, I've consistently encountered the challenge of duplicate ingredients in inventory systems. Despite implementing standardized procedures and regular audits, it's an issue that requires continuous vigilance. Duplicate entries can easily slip through the cracks, leading to confusion, inaccurate stock levels, and ultimately impacting purchasing decisions and cost control. This has taught me that inventory management is an area of ongoing improvement. Keeping a close watch on this aspect of the business is essential for maintaining efficiency and accuracy in our operations.

Techniques:

- Use inventory management software to prevent duplicate entries of ingredients.
- Conduct regular audits to identify and eliminate duplicates, ensuring accurate inventory records.

For example, merging two entries of "flour" into a single consistent entry.

1. Use Generic Item Names:

Instead of creating separate entries for each brand of milk, create a single generic entry for "Milk." This entry will cover all brands and variations.

- **Generic Item:** Milk.
- **Details to Include:** Size, type (whole, skim, etc.), and any other relevant attributes.

2. Same Item with Different Attributes:

When you purchase one item with different attributes, such as Milk 1l / 1.06 qts or Milk 2l / 2.11 qts, or Brand A and Brand B, use the unit conversion rate method instead of entering more than one item on the system.

- **Item Name:** Milk
- **Attributes:** Brand (e.g., Brand A, Brand B), Size (e.g., 1 l / 1.06 qts, 2l / 2.11 qts)

This approach helps in maintaining a cleaner, more organized inventory and avoids the confusion and inefficiencies of managing multiple entries for similar items. This approach also eliminates the need to adjust recipes regularly.

Ingredients

Definition: Ingredient management encompasses sourcing, storing, and using raw materials in a way that balances cost and quality.

Introduction: Effective ingredient management involves securing a reliable supply chain, optimizing storage, and controlling costs to support continuous production without compromising quality. Throughout my career, I've seen how critical it is to establish strong relationships with suppliers and to maintain a well-organized inventory system. One of the lessons I've learned is that consistency in ingredient quality and availability can make or break a restaurant's operation. For instance, there have been times when supply chain disruptions threatened to derail our menu, but because of solid supplier relationships and rigorous inventory control, we were able to navigate these challenges smoothly. By focusing on these fundamentals, I've been able to ensure that our kitchens always have what they need without overstocking or compromising on quality.

Techniques:

- **Supplier Management:** Develop relationships with reliable suppliers to ensure a steady supply of raw materials. Negotiate favorable terms and maintain regular communication to address any supply issues promptly.

- **Inventory Control:** Implement inventory control systems to track raw materials and ensure that stock levels are sufficient to meet production needs without overstocking.

- **Cost Management:** Regularly review and compare supplier prices to ensure that you are getting the best value for your raw materials. Look for opportunities to reduce costs without compromising quality.

- **Storage Optimization:** Store raw materials under optimal conditions to maintain their quality and extend shelf life. Implement FIFO practices to use older stock first.

- **Subcategories:** Build your subcategories according to your business needs. This helps separate between your purchases and identifies high and low-cost inventory items.

Alternative Ingredients

Definition: Alternative ingredients are substitutions that maintain dish quality while potentially lowering costs, which is crucial for flexibility in menu pricing and cost management.

Introduction: Exploring alternative ingredients can be a cost-effective strategy without sacrificing quality, provided these alternatives meet the established standards of the original recipes. In my career, I've often had to navigate the challenge of balancing quality with cost. One particular experience stands out: due to logistical constraints on international shipping, we faced a sudden spike in the price of a key ingredient. Rather than simply absorbing the cost, I led a team in a series of taste tests with various alternative products. We eventually found a substitute that not only maintained the dish's quality but also significantly reduced our costs. This experience reinforced the importance of being adaptable and resourceful when managing food costs.

Techniques:

- Identify and source alternative ingredients that can maintain quality while reducing costs.

- Test these alternatives in recipes for taste and quality and adjust cost calculations accordingly.

  For example, use a different brand of cheese that offers the same quality at a lower price without having to change the recipe. Keep in mind that the ingredient in the recipe remains Cheese.

Semi-Finished Goods

Definition: Semi-finished goods are partially prepared components of dishes that streamline kitchen operations and ensure consistency.

Introduction: Proper management of semi-finished goods reduces preparation time, maintains quality, and ensures efficient use of resources. In my experience, the use of semi-finished goods has been a game-changer, especially in high-volume kitchens where consistency and speed are crucial. I implement this strategy in almost every operation, where we prepare large batches of bases in advance. This not only improves the service speed during peak hours but also enables the operating team to maintain a consistent flavor profile across all dishes. By having these semi-finished products ready, you create the ability to focus on perfecting the final touches, ensuring that every plate meets high standards.

Techniques:

- **Preparation and Storage:** Prepare semi-finished goods in advance and store them under optimal conditions to maintain quality. For example, prepare sauces and bases in bulk and store them in sealed containers.

- **Inventory Tracking:** Use inventory management systems to track the quantity and shelf life of semi-finished goods. Ensure that they are used in a timely manner to prevent spoilage.

- **Quality Control:** Implement strict quality control measures during the preparation and storage of semi-finished goods. Conduct regular checks to ensure consistency and quality.

- **Efficiency:** Use semi-finished goods to streamline the final preparation of dishes, reducing kitchen workload during peak hours and improving service speed.

Finished Goods

Definition: Finished goods are completed products ready for sale, requiring careful management to align with customer demand and minimize waste.

Introduction: Efficient management of finished goods inventory aligns production with demand, minimizes waste, and ensures high-quality offerings are always available to customers. In my career, I developed several franchises, including a coffee shop that served various ready-to-eat pastries and other products as finished goods. We opted to outsource these items because the volumes justified it, and we focused on prolonging the shelf life by sourcing chilled and frozen products that were ready to serve after thawing. This approach not only helped us maintain quality but also ensured we could meet customer demand without unnecessary waste.

Techniques:

- **Forecasting:** Use sales data and demand forecasting to determine the optimal quantity of finished goods to prepare. Adjust production schedules based on expected demand.

- **Inventory Management:** Implement inventory management systems to track finished goods and ensure that stock levels are maintained without overproduction.

- **Quality Assurance:** Conduct regular quality checks on finished goods to ensure they meet the required standards. Address any issues promptly to maintain customer satisfaction.

- **Waste Reduction:** Monitor sales and adjust production quantities to minimize waste. Use promotions and specials to move excess stock before it expires.

Ready to Drink & Ready to Eat

Definition: Ready-to-drink (RTD) and ready-to-eat (RTE) products cater to customer convenience, requiring effective stock management to ensure freshness and availability.

Introduction: Managing ready-to-drink and ready-to-eat products effectively meets customer expectations for convenience and quality, ensuring these products are fresh and available. During my career, I've overseen various operations where RTDs and RTEs played a critical role in meeting customer demand for quick service and convenience. These products are often the go-to choice for busy customers, so ensuring their freshness and availability is key to maintaining customer satisfaction and loyalty.

Techniques:

- **Product Selection:** Choose RTD and RTE products that align with customer preferences and your brand's quality standards. Regularly review and update the selection based on sales data and customer feedback.

- **Inventory Management:** Implement inventory management systems to track the stock levels and shelf life of RTD and RTE products. Ensure timely replenishment to meet demand.

- **Display and Marketing:** Strategically display RTD and RTE products to attract customers. Use promotions and signage to highlight these items and encourage impulse purchases.

- **Quality Control:** Regularly check the quality of RTD and RTE products to ensure they meet safety and quality standards. Remove any expired or damaged items promptly.

Consumables

Definition: Consumables include non-food items like napkins and disposable cutlery, which are integral to the dining experience and require careful cost and stock management.

Introduction: Effective management of consumables like napkins and disposable cutlery ensures operational efficiency and cost control, maintaining adequate stock levels without over-ordering. Throughout my career, I've seen how even small items like napkins or straws can have a significant impact on the overall cost structure if not managed properly. It's the attention to these details that often separates successful operations from the rest, ensuring that everything runs smoothly without unnecessary overspending.

Techniques:

- **Inventory Management:** Implement an inventory management system to track consumable items. Set par levels to ensure consistent availability without overstocking.

- **Usage Monitoring:** Monitor the usage of consumables to identify patterns and adjust ordering quantities accordingly. Use this data to prevent waste and reduce costs.

- **Supplier Relationships:** Develop relationships with reliable suppliers to ensure a steady supply of consumables. Negotiate favorable terms and bulk purchase discounts where possible.

- **Cost Control:** Regularly review and compare prices from different suppliers to ensure you are getting the best value. Implement cost-saving measures, such as using more cost-effective alternatives or reducing usage.

Guest Supplies

Definition: Guest supplies such as toiletries and linens enhance the customer experience, necessitating meticulous control over quality and stock levels.

Introduction: Ensuring a consistent supply of guest supplies is crucial for enhancing the customer experience, requiring careful inventory management and quality control. Over the years, I've learned that the smallest details, like the quality of linens or the availability of toiletries, can significantly impact a guest's perception of your business. It's this attention to detail that turns a one-time visitor into a loyal customer, making the management of guest supplies a vital aspect of operations.

Techniques:

- **Inventory Control:** Use an inventory management system to track guest supplies and maintain optimal stock levels. Set reorder points to prevent stockouts.

- **Quality Assurance:** Regularly check the quality of guest supplies to ensure they meet your standards. Replace any items that do not meet quality expectations.

- **Supplier Management:** Develop strong relationships with suppliers to ensure timely delivery of high-quality guest supplies. Negotiate favorable terms and monitor supplier performance.

- **Customer Feedback:** Collect and analyze customer feedback on guest supplies to identify areas for improvement. Use this feedback to make informed decisions about product selection and quality.

Cleaning & Sanitary Products

Definition: Cleaning and sanitary products are crucial for maintaining hygiene standards in restaurant operations, requiring strict inventory control and usage monitoring.

Introduction: Over the years, I've come to realize that maintaining impeccable hygiene standards isn't just about having the right cleaning products; it's about ensuring those products are used correctly and consistently. Effective management of cleaning and sanitary products is vital for meeting health regulations and ensuring a safe, clean environment for both customers and staff. This requires not just regular checks but also ongoing training and a strong relationship with suppliers.

Techniques:

- **Inventory Management:** Implement an inventory management system to track cleaning and sanitary products. Set par levels to ensure consistent availability and compliance with health regulations.

- **Quality Control:** Regularly review the effectiveness and quality of cleaning products. Ensure they meet health and safety standards and replace any substandard products.

- **Training:** Train staff on the proper use of cleaning and sanitary products to ensure effective hygiene practices. Provide regular updates on new products and techniques.

- **Supplier Relationships:** Work with reliable suppliers to ensure a steady supply of high-quality cleaning and sanitary products. Negotiate favorable terms and monitor supplier performance.

Inventory Storage

What is Inventory Storage?

Inventory storage in restaurant management involves the careful organization and maintenance of all food, beverage, and non-food items to preserve their quality, ensure safety, and maximize shelf life. This includes the proper arrangement of goods in designated areas such as refrigerators, freezers, dry storage, and shelving units. Effective inventory storage is crucial for preventing contamination, minimizing waste, and managing costs by ensuring that ingredients are used efficiently and within their best-before periods.

Why is Inventory Storage Critical?

Effective inventory storage is a cornerstone of successful restaurant management, ensuring that ingredients are kept in optimal conditions to preserve freshness, prevent spoilage, and maintain quality. During my time as a regional manager in MENA, we partnered with a third-party logistics company to store our imported pastries at -20 degrees Celsius (-4 degrees Fahrenheit). We had specific SOPs in place for them to gradually thaw the products, and they received training on this sensitive process. However, during our first inspection, we discovered that the pastries were stored under chilled conditions instead of the required frozen state. This oversight led to a significant loss of $20,000 worth of product, which had to be discarded. This experience highlighted the critical importance of proper labeling and strict adherence to storage instructions. Proper inventory storage not only supports efficient kitchen operations but also plays a crucial role in cost control by reducing waste and extending the usable life of ingredients.

Multiple Storage within a Kitchen and Restaurant

Restaurant kitchens often face the challenge of efficiently managing a diverse range of ingredients, which can easily lead to clutter and operational inefficiencies if not well-organized. Throughout my career, I've seen firsthand how disorganization in the kitchen can slow down service and increase waste. One key lesson I've learned is the importance of compartmentalizing storage areas to optimize both accessibility and inventory tracking.

To combat this, it's crucial that you:

- **Organize your inventory** in different storage areas based on usage and type. This segregation helps you reduce time spent on searching for items and improves the speed of service.

- **Use clear labeling and inventory management systems** to keep track of stock in each area, ensuring quick accessibility and accurate tracking.

  For example, in one of the restaurants I managed, we maintained separate storage areas for dry goods, refrigerated items, and frozen foods, each clearly labeled. This simple yet effective system streamlined our operations and minimized confusion, significantly improving our kitchen's efficiency.

Storage State (Chilled, Frozen, Ambient, etc.)

The state in which food is stored directly impacts its quality and safety, two pillars of successful kitchen management.

To ensure optimal storage conditions:

- **Store ingredients at appropriate temperatures** to maintain quality and extend shelf life.

- **Regularly monitor and record storage temperatures** and implement FIFO (First In, First Out) practices to minimize waste.

  For example, in one of the kitchens I oversaw, we always anticipated the time needed to thaw frozen products and planned our preparations in reverse. This approach not only optimized ingredient usage but also significantly reduced waste, ensuring that we served the freshest, highest-quality dishes possible.

Central Storage

Centralizing storage can significantly streamline operations by reducing the time staff spend fetching items and by lowering costs through bulk purchasing. In my experience, central storage is not just about convenience—it's about creating an efficient, well-organized system that supports the entire kitchen's workflow.

Implementing a central storage system allows:

- **Centralize bulk storage** for high-use items to streamline inventory management and reduce costs. This was a game-changer in one of the operations I managed, where we saw a noticeable improvement in efficiency and cost savings.

- **Implement a system for tracking inventory movement** between central storage and kitchen areas to ensure smooth operations. This level of organization helped maintain a clean and organized kitchen environment, which is essential for running a successful restaurant.

  For example, we centralized bulk storage of rice in one location and scheduled regular transfers to the kitchen. This simple adjustment not only kept the kitchen more organized but also freed up staff to focus on food preparation rather than constantly retrieving supplies.

Central Production (for larger business)

In larger operations, managing preparations across multiple locations can quickly become chaotic. To tackle this, I've found that establishing a central production facility is key to maintaining order and consistency across the board.

By utilizing a central production facility, you can:

- **Prepare ingredients or semi-finished products** for multiple outlets, which not only improves consistency but also reduces waste and lowers labor costs. This approach has been a cornerstone in some of the larger operations I've managed, where it significantly streamlined processes and ensured that each outlet maintained the same high standards.

  For example, in one of my roles, we prepared sauces in bulk at a central kitchen and distributed them to various locations. This ensured that the quality remained consistent, and the operational efficiency was greatly enhanced, as each outlet could focus more on service and less on preparation.

Central Kitchen (for larger business)

A central kitchen is the beating heart of any multi-outlet culinary operation, ensuring that every dish served across various locations meets the same high standard of quality and consistency. In my experience, implementing a central kitchen not only streamlines production but also significantly enhances operational efficiency.

By operating a central kitchen, you can:

- **Produce menu items for multiple outlets,** guaranteeing consistency and efficiency across the board. This was particularly effective in a large-scale operation I managed, where we centralized bread production.

- **Standardize recipes and processes** to maintain the same quality across all locations. For instance, by baking bread in a central kitchen and delivering it to various restaurants, we ensured product uniformity while reducing the workload in individual kitchens. This allowed the restaurant staff to focus on what truly matters—crafting exceptional dining experiences for guests.

Inventory Movement

Definition: Inventory movement refers to the processes involved in managing the flow of goods within a restaurant, from receiving and storage to usage and waste disposal. Effective inventory movement ensures that all items are efficiently utilized, minimizing waste and optimizing stock levels.

Introduction: Over the years, I've learned that effective inventory movement is not just about tracking items; it's about maintaining a rhythm in the kitchen that ensures smooth operations and cost control. In one of my previous roles, I encountered significant challenges with inventory management, where products were often lost in the transition between storage and the kitchen. By implementing stricter controls and clearer processes, we managed to reduce waste significantly and keep a closer eye on stock levels. Effective inventory movement involves managing the flow of goods from storage to use, ensuring that every item is accounted for, from incoming deliveries to final dish preparation. This section explains strategies to streamline this process, helping you maintain control over your inventory and reduce operational costs.

Forecast & Demand Planning

Definition: Forecasting and demand planning involve predicting future inventory needs based on historical sales data and market trends to align stock levels with business demands.

Introduction: One of the lessons I've learned over the years is the critical role that accurate forecasting plays in inventory management. Early in my career, I faced challenges with overstocking certain items, leading to unnecessary waste and inflated costs. By closely analyzing historical sales data and market trends, we were able to refine our purchasing strategies significantly. Utilizing historical sales data and market trends helps anticipate the demand for each menu item, ensuring efficient stock management and minimizing both shortages and excess inventory.

Techniques:

- Use sales data to forecast demand for each menu item.
- Adjust purchasing and production schedules based on these forecasts to maintain optimal stock levels and reduce waste.

  For example, if data shows increased demand for salads during summer, adjust orders for fresh vegetables accordingly.

Par Levels

Definition: Par levels are the minimum stock quantities required to meet expected demand without overstocking, ensuring continuous operation.

Introduction: Early in my career, I learned the importance of setting the right par levels after experiencing firsthand the chaos that ensues from both overstocking and running out of key ingredients during peak times. Properly setting and maintaining par levels is a delicate balance that, when done right, ensures smooth operations and cost control.

Techniques:

- Set par levels for each inventory item based on average usage and lead time for reordering.
- Regularly review and adjust par levels to reflect changes in sales patterns.
- Use inventory management systems to automate alerts when the stock falls below par levels.

Transfers

Definition: Transfers involve the movement of inventory items between different locations or storage areas within a restaurant to ensure availability where needed.

Introduction: I've seen how critical proper transfer management can be, especially in larger operations where multiple kitchens and storage areas are involved. Mismanaged transfers can lead to inventory discrepancies, confusion among staff, and ultimately, a breakdown in service. Efficient management of transfers is key to maintaining accurate inventory records and ensuring that items are available in the necessary areas without delay.

Techniques:

- Track transfers of ingredients and products between different storage areas or locations using inventory management software.
- Ensure accurate record-keeping to maintain inventory accuracy and accountability.

  For example, recording the transfer of vegetables from central storage to the kitchen.

Logging Waste

Definition: Waste logging is the practice of recording unused or spoiled inventory items to identify loss points and implement corrective measures.

Introduction: Waste is an inevitable part of any restaurant operation, but how you manage and learn from it can make all the difference. In my career, I've learned that regularly logging and analyzing waste is not just about reducing costs—it's about fostering a culture of efficiency and sustainability within the team. By identifying where waste occurs, we can implement targeted strategies that not only save money but also enhance our operational effectiveness.

Techniques:

- Implement a system for logging waste to identify patterns and implement waste reduction strategies.

- Analyze waste logs to determine causes of waste and take corrective actions.

  For example, recording and analyzing waste from overproduction or spoilage.

Batch Logging Systems & Production Cycles

Definition: Batch logging involves recording detailed information about each batch of product made, including ingredients, usage, and production dates, to ensure traceability and quality control.

Introduction: Over the years, I've come to appreciate the importance of meticulous batch logging, especially in high-volume production environments. A comprehensive batch logging system not only enhances transparency across the production cycle but also plays a crucial role in maintaining consistency, quality control, and minimizing waste. It also ensures accurate production costing, which is vital for maintaining profitability. For example, when a central kitchen produces a large batch of croissants, it's essential to log each step to accurately deplete inventory and calculate the cost per portion, ensuring that every unit sold is profitable.

Techniques:

- Implement a batch logging system where each batch of production is recorded with details like ingredients used, yield, and production date.

- This helps in tracking ingredient usage, ensuring quality control, and reducing waste.

  For example, log each batch of soup produced with the date, quantity, and ingredients used.

Part Four:
Administration and Control

Administration and Control

Effective administration and control are an essence of successful restaurant management. Over the years, I've seen firsthand how meticulous management practices can turn around even the most challenging operations. This chapter delves into the critical aspects of managing your restaurant's operations with precision and efficiency, drawing from both industry standards and personal experience. From requisitioning supplies to conducting comprehensive financial analysis, it covers the essential strategies needed to streamline operations, reduce costs, and enhance profitability.

In my career, I've learned that the success of a restaurant often hinges on how well you manage the behind-the-scenes details. Whether it was in a high-pressure role managing a multinational food operation or a more intimate setting in a local eatery, the principles of strong administration and control have always been paramount. This section will guide you through the techniques for inventory management, supplier negotiations, and the implementation of cutting-edge technology that I've found most effective. These tools are designed to optimize every facet of your restaurant's operations, ensuring that your establishment not only meets but exceeds the demands of the competitive food service industry.

Prepare to enhance your managerial capabilities and apply these insights to create a more streamlined, efficient, and profitable business.

Price Locking in Inventory Management Systems

Price locking is a critical feature in Restaurant Operating Systems (ROS) and Inventory Management Systems (IMS) that ensures the cost of ingredients remains consistent with pre-negotiated supplier agreements. I've experienced firsthand how a minor oversight in pricing can have a significant impact on food costs, which is why this functionality is so crucial. By preventing the accidental acceptance of goods at higher prices than agreed upon, price locking plays a key role in maintaining cost control and protecting profitability.

How Price Locking Works

- **Contractual Agreements:** It all starts with negotiating the right prices with suppliers. These prices are then locked into the system, ensuring there are no surprises down the line.

- **System Integration:** The ROS or IMS is configured to reflect these agreed prices and will flag any discrepancies at the time of receiving goods. This has saved me from potential cost overruns on more than one occasion.

- **Receiving Process:** When inventory arrives, the system checks the invoice against the locked price. If there's a mismatch, the system alerts the receiver, prompting immediate resolution before acceptance.

Benefits of Price Locking

- **Cost Control:** By keeping the cost of goods stable, you maintain consistent food cost percentages, a lesson I've learned is vital for long-term profitability.

- **Budget Predictability:** This feature has been invaluable in helping me plan and budget effectively, preventing unexpected spikes in ingredient costs.

- **Dispute Resolution:** When there's a discrepancy, having the agreed prices documented and enforced by the system provides a solid foundation for resolving any issues with suppliers.

Implementing Price Locking in an IMS

- **Supplier Setup:** Make sure all supplier contracts are accurately reflected in the IMS with the correct prices and terms. This step is crucial to avoid any discrepancies.

- **Staff Training:** It's essential to train your receiving and procurement teams on the importance of price locking and how to handle any discrepancies. In my experience, this training prevents costly mistakes.

- **Regular Updates:** Regularly reviewing and updating price locking setups ensures that your system remains accurate and reflects any new contracts or changes in supplier terms.

Requisitions

Definition: Requisitions are internal requests for ingredients or supplies, critical for maintaining control and ensuring accountability in inventory management.

Introduction: In my career, I've found that a well-structured requisition system is vital for ensuring the smooth flow of operations. Implementing a robust requisition process not only enhances efficiency but also helps in maintaining control over your internal supply chains, from request submission to order fulfillment. This system ensures that nothing slips through the cracks, and every ingredient or supply is accounted for.

Techniques:

1. **Standard Procedures:** One of the first steps I always take is developing and documenting standard procedures for internal requisitions. This includes clear approval processes and detailed documentation requirements, which help avoid any confusion or bottlenecks.

2. **Tracking:** In today's digital age, I strongly advocate using digital tools or software to track requisitions from the moment they are submitted until they are fulfilled. This ensures that each request is logged and approved by the appropriate personnel, providing a clear trail that can be referenced at any time.

3. **Accountability:** It's essential to assign responsibility for approving and fulfilling requisitions to specific staff members. This not only ensures accountability but also empowers your team by giving them ownership of their roles.

4. **Audits:** Regular audits of requisition records are non-negotiable in my book. They help ensure compliance with established procedures and allow you to identify and correct any discrepancies before they become bigger issues.

Purchase Orders

Definition: Purchase orders are formal documents issued by a buyer to a supplier, specifying the products or services agreed upon for purchase at a set price.

Introduction: Throughout my career, I've seen how a well-managed purchase order system can significantly streamline procurement processes and reduce errors. Standardizing purchase orders not only simplifies communication between your restaurant and suppliers but also helps ensure that everyone is on the same page, preventing costly misunderstandings.

Techniques:

- **Standardization:** One of my first steps in any operation is to standardize the purchase order process. By using templates and digital tools, you can ensure consistency and accuracy, which are critical in maintaining a smooth procurement process.

- **Approval Workflow:** Establish a clear approval workflow for purchase orders. This ensures that all orders are reviewed and approved by authorized personnel before they are placed, minimizing errors and unauthorized spending.

- **Communication:** Clear communication with suppliers is key. I make it a point to ensure that all order details—quantities, specifications, and delivery dates—are communicated clearly and confirmed with the supplier to avoid any discrepancies.

- **Record Keeping:** Over the years, I've learned the importance of meticulous record keeping. Maintaining detailed records of all purchase orders and related documents, like delivery notes and invoices, not only helps in future reference but is also crucial during audits.

GRN (Goods Received Note)

Definition: A Goods Received Note (GRN) is a document that officially records the receipt of goods from a supplier, detailing the specifics and quantities delivered to ensure accuracy and accountability.

Introduction: In my experience, the process of issuing GRNs is indispensable for maintaining precise inventory records and verifying that what you receive matches what was ordered. It's a crucial step in the supply chain that helps prevent discrepancies and ensure that inventory levels reflect actual stock.

Techniques:

- **Verification:** Over the years, I've emphasized the importance of thorough verification upon delivery. Checking the received goods against the purchase order and delivery note for quantities, price, specifications, and quality is the first line of defense against inventory discrepancies.

- **Documentation:** Issuing a detailed GRN is not just a formality but a critical step in documenting the receipt of goods. By including specifics like item descriptions, quantities, and any discrepancies, you create a clear record that supports both inventory accuracy and financial tracking.

- **Inventory Update:** I've always advocated for real-time inventory updates based on the GRN. Using inventory management software to streamline this process ensures that your stock levels are always accurate, which is essential for both daily operations and long-term planning.

- **Discrepancy Management:** In my career, I've encountered discrepancies more often than I'd like. Promptly addressing these differences and communicating with suppliers to resolve them is vital. Documenting these resolutions helps prevent future issues and maintains a strong relationship with your suppliers.

Three Step Verification

Definition: Three-step verification is a procurement process that involves cross-checking purchase orders, delivery notes, and invoices to ensure transaction accuracy and prevent discrepancies.

Introduction: Over the years, I've found that implementing a three-step verification process is not just about safeguarding against errors but also about building a robust system of accountability. This methodical approach is crucial in ensuring that every transaction aligns with both operational needs and financial controls.

Techniques:

- **Step 1: Purchase Order:** The foundation of any procurement process starts with creating and approving a detailed purchase order. From my experience, it's essential to ensure that all details—quantities, specifications, and pricing—are meticulously accurate and authorized by the appropriate personnel before proceeding.

- **Step 2: Delivery Note:** Upon receipt of goods, I always stress the importance of verifying the delivery note against the purchase order. This step is where you confirm that what was ordered is exactly what was received, in terms of quantity, specifications, and quality.

- **Step 3: Invoice:** The final check involves verifying the supplier's invoice against both the purchase order and the delivery note. Ensuring all details match and that the goods received are as ordered is critical for maintaining accurate financial records and preventing overpayments.

- **Reconciliation:** In practice, discrepancies can and do occur. I've learned that prompt reconciliation of any differences between the purchase order, delivery note, and invoice is essential. Documenting the resolution and updating both inventory and financial records ensures that your books are accurate and that any issues are addressed before they become bigger problems.

Physical Stock Count

Definition: Physical stock counts are essential audits that involve physically verifying the quantities and conditions of items in storage to ensure the accuracy of inventory records.

Introduction: In my career, I've always emphasized the importance of regular physical stock counts. These audits are more than just a routine task; they are a critical checkpoint to ensure that what's on paper matches what's on the shelves. Accurate stock counts can prevent financial losses and help avoid operational inefficiencies that arise from discrepancies in inventory records.

Techniques:

- **Regular Scheduling:** I've found that scheduling physical counts at regular intervals—whether monthly, quarterly, or based on business needs—helps maintain ongoing accuracy in your inventory records. This proactive approach reduces the risk of major discrepancies building up over time.

- **Reconciliation:** After the physical count, reconciling the results with the theoretical inventory levels in your management system is crucial. This step ensures that your records reflect the actual stock levels, allowing for adjustments that prevent potential financial inaccuracies.

- **Training:** Training staff on proper counting techniques is something I've always prioritized. Accurate reporting during stock counts not only improves data reliability but also instills a culture of precision and accountability within the team.

I've implemented monthly stock counts of all ingredients in the operations I've managed. This practice has been key to reconciling inventory records with actual stock, ensuring that any discrepancies are identified and resolved promptly, thus maintaining the integrity of the inventory management system.

Manual Cost Control Template

Definition: A manual cost control template is a fundamental tool designed to track and analyze daily expenses and sales, providing a clear view of a restaurant's financial performance and helping to manage costs effectively.

Introduction: Throughout my career, especially in the earlier days before fully integrated systems were the norm, I relied heavily on manual cost control templates. Even today, these templates play a vital role as a backup and verification tool to confirm the data recorded in the IMS. They're not just about tracking numbers; they provide an additional layer of accuracy and assurance in understanding a restaurant's financial health. By diligently logging and analyzing data manually, I could cross-check and validate the IMS figures, ensuring we had a true picture of our financial performance.

Techniques:

- **Daily Logging:** In my experience, the key to effective cost management starts with consistency. I've always ensured that my teams maintain daily logs of ingredient usage and sales. This daily discipline allows us to monitor trends closely and catch inefficiencies before they become bigger issues.
- **Analysis:** Regular analysis of the data collected through these templates has been crucial in my approach. By spotting patterns and assessing financial performance regularly, I've been able to make informed decisions that directly improve cost control and operational efficiency.

- **Customization:** I've learned that one size doesn't fit all when it comes to cost control. Customizing the template to fit the specific needs of each restaurant or operation is something I've always advocated for. This ensures that every relevant cost is tracked, providing a comprehensive view of the business's financial landscape.

For example, I've often used a simple spreadsheet to log daily ingredient usage and sales. By comparing actual expenses against budgeted costs, I could pinpoint where efficiency improvements were needed, leading to significant cost savings over time.

Inventory Audits and Spot Checks

The Rational

Throughout my career, I've seen how easily inventory discrepancies can spiral out of control if not caught early. Regular spot checks and inventory audits are critical tools that have helped me maintain a tight grip on inventory management, ensuring that stock levels are accurate and that the business remains profitable. These audits aren't just routine—they're a proactive measure to safeguard the integrity of your operations:

1. **Highly Consumed Items in the Inventory**

   - **Why:** These items are the backbone of daily operations. If there's one thing I've learned, it's that running out of a key ingredient during a busy service can bring everything to a standstill. Monitoring these items closely helps avoid stockouts and overstocking, which can lead to wastage or lost sales.

   - **What to Look For:** Compare actual inventory counts with usage reports. Ensure that the high consumption rate aligns with sales and production records. If I noticed a mismatch in past audits, it often pointed to unrecorded usage or inefficiencies that needed immediate correction.

2. **High-Cost Items**

   - **Why:** High-cost items have a direct impact on your bottom line. I've experienced firsthand how even minor discrepancies in these items can lead to significant financial losses. That's why they deserve special attention during audits.

   - **What to Look For:** Verify the count and condition of high-cost items. In my audits, I've always checked for signs of pilferage, spoilage, or mismanagement. Keeping a close eye on these items can prevent costly errors and maintain profitability.

3. **Packaging Materials Count**

   - **Why:** Packaging materials might seem insignificant, but in high-volume operations, they contribute considerably to operational expenses and product presentation. I've seen how overlooked packaging costs can eat into profits.

   - **What to Look For:** Check for adequate stock levels of packaging materials and ensure they are stored properly to prevent damage. In my experience, especially with high-volume takeaway restaurants, comparing usage rates against sales has been key to detecting any anomalies, such as excessive usage or mismanagement.

4. **Units of Measurements and Conversion Rates**

   - **Why:** Accurate units of measurement are the foundation of reliable inventory tracking and cost control. I've always stressed the importance of consistency in this area to avoid costly mistakes.

   - **What to Look For:** Ensure that inventory items are recorded using the correct units of measurement. When I've audited inventory, I've verified that conversion rates between different units (e.g., cases to individual units) are accurate and consistently applied, preventing discrepancies that could skew financial reports.

5. **Unusual High Numbers in Inventory Reports**

   - **Why:** Unusually high or low inventory numbers are red flags. Over the years,

I've learned that these anomalies often signal underlying issues such as errors, theft, or even systematic failures.

- **What to Look For:** Scrutinize inventory reports for unusually high or low quantities and values. Whenever I've encountered such discrepancies, I've made it a point to cross-reference with purchase orders, delivery notes, and sales records to get to the root of the problem.

The Procedure

Conducting spot checks and audits with a systematic approach not only ensures accuracy but also streamlines the process, making it more efficient and less disruptive to operations. Over the years, I've honed a procedure that balances thoroughness with practicality.

1. **Select a Sample:** When conducting a spot check, it's crucial to choose a representative sample of inventory items. I always focus on highly consumed items, high-cost items, and packaging materials because these are the most likely to show discrepancies if something is amiss.

2. **Count and Compare:** Physically counting the selected items and comparing these counts to inventory records—what I often refer to as Actual vs. Theoretical—has been a game-changer. This step helps identify gaps between what's recorded and what's actually in stock. In my experience, this comparison often uncovers discrepancies that would otherwise go unnoticed.

3. **Investigate Discrepancies:** If there are discrepancies, digging into the causes is essential. I've found that checking recent transactions, delivery notes, and usage logs often reveals where things went wrong. It could be anything from a simple recording error to a more serious issue like theft or mismanagement.

4. **Adjust Records:** Once the discrepancies are identified, adjusting the inventory records to reflect accurate counts is crucial. In my audits, I've always ensured that any corrections made are thoroughly documented. This not only keeps the records accurate but also creates a paper trail that can be invaluable for future reference.

5. **Report Findings:** Finally, preparing a detailed report of the spot check's findings is vital. I make sure to include any discrepancies, their potential causes, and the corrective actions taken. This report serves as a record for future audits and helps in continuously improving the process.

Regular spot checks and audits are more than just a routine task; they are a safeguard for your inventory and financial health. By focusing on key areas such as highly consumed items, high-cost items, and packaging materials, and following a clear procedure, you can promptly identify and address issues, ensuring that your inventory remains accurate and your business stays on solid financial footing.

Part Five

Recipes and Production Management

Recipes and Production Management

Throughout my career, I've seen firsthand the critical role that recipe and production management plays in a restaurant's success. Whether it was during my time running a bustling kitchen in Algeria or optimizing operations at a high-end dining establishment in Sydney, the principles of standardization, efficiency, and consistency have always been at the forefront of my approach. The strategies and techniques in this section are not just theoretical; they are battle-tested methods that I've implemented across various culinary landscapes to ensure quality and profitability. Let's dive into these essential aspects of kitchen management, where precision meets creativity, and see how they can transform your operations.

Product Recipe

Definition: Product recipes are standardized instructions for preparing each menu item, ensuring consistency in taste, appearance, and cost.

Introduction: When I first started refining recipes for my restaurant concept in Algeria, the importance of having standardized recipes became immediately apparent. Without them, consistency wavered, and customer satisfaction dipped. I quickly learned that a detailed, standardized recipe is the backbone of any successful kitchen. It was this realization that drove me to implement recipe management software, ensuring that every dish met the same high standards, no matter who was in the kitchen.

Techniques:

- **Recipe Management Software:** Utilize software to maintain and update recipes, ensuring changes are documented and communicated to all relevant staff.

- **Standardization:** Ensure all menu items have a standardized recipe that includes detailed ingredient quantities and preparation steps.

For example, create a job aid sheet for lasagna that includes a standardized recipe, ensuring every serving is consistent.

Batch Recipe

Definition: Batch recipes are standardized procedures for preparing large quantities of a product, ensuring uniform quality and efficiency.

Introduction: During my tenure with a popular chocolate concept in Abu Dhabi, we had a high-demand hot chocolate that required batch production to keep up with the rush. The challenge was to maintain the same rich flavor and texture across every batch, which led me to meticulously document and standardize our batch recipes. This not only streamlined operations but also ensured that our customers enjoyed the same quality every time, regardless of how busy we were. Creating batch recipes is essential for large-scale production, improving consistency while optimizing resource usage.

Techniques:

- **Documentation:** Document batch recipes in detail and ensure they are accessible to all kitchen staff.
- **Training:** Train staff to follow batch recipes precisely to avoid variations in product quality.

  For example, a batch recipe for soup that specifies quantities for producing 30 servings.

Sub Recipe

Definition: Sub recipes are recipes for components that are used in multiple dishes, helping streamline kitchen operations and maintain consistency.

Introduction: In the fast-paced environment of a Miami concept I created, sub-recipes became a game-changer. By creating detailed sub-recipes for sauces and other base components, we were able to maintain consistent flavor profiles across multiple dishes. This approach not only enhanced efficiency but also allowed us to scale up production without sacrificing quality. Developing sub-recipes for commonly used components can greatly enhance kitchen efficiency and standardization.

Techniques:

- **Integration:** Incorporate sub-recipes into main dishes to ensure consistent flavor and quality across menu items.
- **Documentation:** Keep detailed records of all sub-recipes and update them as needed.

  For example, a sub-recipe for a sauce used in several different pasta dishes to ensure uniform taste and quality.

Production Cycle

Definition: The production cycle involves planning and managing the sequence of tasks from ingredient prep to final dish assembly to optimize kitchen workflow.

Introduction: Managing the production cycle effectively was crucial during my time as a regional manager overseeing multiple outlets in the MENA region. By scheduling production activities around peak demand times and ingredient availability, we were able to minimize waste and ensure that our kitchens were always prepared for the busiest service periods. Regular reviews and adjustments kept us agile and responsive to the ever-changing dynamics of the restaurant industry. Effective management of the production cycle reduces waste, ensures the timely availability of dishes, and enhances overall operational efficiency.

Techniques:

- **Scheduling:** Plan production activities based on demand forecasts and ingredient availability to minimize downtime and waste.
- **Monitoring:** Regularly review and adjust the production cycle to respond to real-time kitchen dynamics.

For example, organize the daily production schedule for bakery items to align with peak sales times.

Expiration Date

Definition: Expiration date monitoring involves tracking the shelf life of perishable items to ensure they are used before becoming unsuitable for consumption.

Introduction: Expiration date monitoring became a critical part of our operations when I was running a coffee shop chain that also sold retail products. Implementing an inventory management system that tracked expiry dates allowed us to rotate stock efficiently, reducing waste and ensuring that we were always serving the freshest products. This system also helped us stay ahead of potential losses by setting up alerts for upcoming expiries, enabling proactive management.

Techniques:

- Use inventory management systems to track expiry dates and reduce waste by ensuring timely usage of perishable items.
- Implement alerts for upcoming expiries and prioritize using older stock.
  For example, rotating stock to use items nearing their expiry date first.

Tools and Equipment

Definition: Tools and equipment in a kitchen include all hardware used to prepare, cook, and store food, which must be maintained to support efficient operations.

Introduction: The importance of investing in high-quality tools and equipment was a lesson I learned early in my career. At one of my first managerial positions, we struggled with frequent equipment failures that disrupted service. By advocating for and eventually securing higher-quality tools, we not only improved kitchen efficiency but also saw a reduction in downtime and maintenance costs. Training staff on proper usage and maintenance further extended the lifespan of our equipment, making it a worthwhile investment. Investing in the right tools and maintaining them properly increases kitchen efficiency, reduces waste, and ensures food safety.

Techniques:

- **Invest in Quality Equipment**: Purchase high-quality kitchen tools and equipment that can withstand regular use. This includes precision scales, portioning tools, and temperature control devices.

- **Maintenance**: Regularly maintain and calibrate equipment to ensure it remains accurate and efficient. Schedule routine checks and servicing.

- **Training**: Provide comprehensive training for staff on how to use and maintain kitchen equipment properly. Create user manuals and training videos if necessary.

- **Evaluation**: Regularly assess the performance of tools and equipment. Replace or upgrade as needed to maintain efficiency and quality.

Utensils and Their Importance in the Food Cost

Definition: Utensils are the tools used for measuring, preparing, and serving food, and their proper use is crucial for controlling food costs.

Introduction: In one of the kitchens I managed, inconsistent use of measuring utensils was leading to significant variances in food costs. I implemented a system where each station was equipped with standardized measuring tools, and staff were trained on their proper use. This simple change brought our food costs under control and ensured that every dish was served as intended, both in portion size and profitability.

Techniques:

- **Standardize Utensils**: Use standardized measuring utensils for ingredients and portion control. Ensure that every kitchen station is equipped with the necessary tools.

- **Consistency:** Ensure all staff use the same utensils for measuring and portioning to maintain consistency in servings and ingredient usage.

- **Training:** Train staff on the proper use of measuring and portioning utensils. Emphasize the impact on food costs and consistency.

- **Audits:** Conduct regular audits to ensure utensils are being used correctly and consistently. Provide feedback and additional training if discrepancies are found.

Part Six:

Purchasing and Procurement

Purchasing and Procurement

Purchasing and procurement involve the strategic processes of sourcing, acquiring, and managing the goods and services necessary for restaurant operations. This includes everything from negotiating supplier contracts to ensuring the timely delivery of high-quality ingredients and supplies at optimal costs.

Throughout my career, I've had the privilege of setting up new markets across the globe—Australia, the Middle East, the USA, Europe, and Africa. Each region brought its unique challenges and opportunities, particularly when it came to establishing a reliable and efficient supply chain. My experience with adapting and implementing franchise concepts from the US and Europe into the MENA region taught me the critical importance of purchasing and procurement. From scratch, I was often tasked with developing supply chains that met both the quality standards of the brand and the logistical realities of the local market.

Navigating these complexities has been a cornerstone of my work, whether it was finding the right suppliers, negotiating favorable terms, or ensuring that the supply chain was resilient enough to handle the demands of a bustling restaurant environment. This part of the book will delve into the techniques and strategies that have been crucial in my journey, offering insights on how to effectively manage procurement processes to maintain both cost control and quality. Whether you're expanding into a new market or refining operations in an established one, these strategies are designed to help you optimize your purchasing and procurement processes, ensuring your restaurant's success.

Supplier Management

Definition: Supplier management involves the processes of selecting, setting up, and managing relationships with suppliers to ensure a steady supply of quality goods at optimal prices.

Introduction: In my extensive experience across various global markets, the importance of robust supplier management cannot be overstated. Establishing strong, reliable supplier relationships has been a key factor in ensuring consistent quality and service in every restaurant I've managed or set up. Whether it was sourcing fresh produce for a new concept in the Middle East or securing the best coffee beans for a chain in Miami, the ability to negotiate favorable terms and maintain ongoing communication with suppliers has been vital.

Through careful selection and rigorous performance reviews, I've learned that effective supplier management is not just about getting the best price—it's about building partnerships that support the long-term success of the restaurant.

Techniques:

- **Criteria for Selection:** Establish criteria for selecting suppliers that focus on quality, reliability, and cost to ensure a consistent supply of ingredients.

- **Negotiate Terms:** Set up accounts and negotiate terms with suppliers before placing orders to secure favorable conditions.

- **Building Relationship:** Foster strong, long-term relationships with suppliers to create partnerships based on trust and mutual benefit. Regular communication and collaboration can lead to better service, preferential terms, and more flexibility.

- **Performance Review:** Regularly review and communicate with suppliers to ensure they meet the agreed standards of quality and pricing, adjusting as needed for any changes in restaurant needs or market conditions.

Price Lock

Definition: Price locking involves negotiating fixed prices with suppliers for a specific period to mitigate the risk of price fluctuations.

Introduction: I've seen firsthand the impact that fluctuating ingredient costs can have on a restaurant's profitability. In dynamic markets, price volatility can quickly erode profit margins if not managed carefully. Price locking has been one of the most effective strategies I've employed to maintain control over food costs, particularly when managing large-scale operations or during periods of economic uncertainty. By securing fixed prices for key ingredients, I've been able to stabilize menu costs, ensuring that we can deliver consistent pricing to customers while protecting the bottom line. This proactive approach not only simplifies budgeting but also strengthens supplier relationships, as it demonstrates a commitment to long-term partnerships.

Techniques:

- **Negotiate Fixed Prices:** Secure fixed prices with suppliers for essential ingredients over a set period, such as six months, to prevent unexpected cost increases that could affect your pricing structure and margins.

- **Compliance Monitoring:** Document these agreements meticulously and regularly review supplier invoices to ensure that the locked prices are being honored. This ongoing vigilance helps prevent any discrepancies that could slip through unnoticed.

  For example, locking in the price of chicken for six months can stabilize menu costs, protecting your restaurant from sudden spikes in the cost of this staple ingredient, thereby ensuring pricing consistency for your customers.

Negotiations

Definition: Negotiations with suppliers are critical for securing favorable terms and prices, involving strategic preparation and relationship management.

Introduction: Negotiating with suppliers has always been more than just a transactional process for me—it's about building partnerships that can withstand the test of time and market fluctuations. Over the years, I've learned that successful negotiations are rooted in thorough preparation and a deep understanding of both your own needs and the supplier's capabilities. Whether I was setting up supply chains in new markets or adapting global franchise concepts to local environments, the ability to negotiate effectively made a significant difference in managing costs and ensuring a reliable supply of quality ingredients. A well-negotiated agreement not only enhances your bottom line but also fosters a sense of mutual respect and cooperation that can lead to long-term benefits for both parties.

Strategy:

- **Preparation:** Before entering any negotiation, I always invest time in researching market prices and clearly defining our procurement needs. This preparation is crucial as it strengthens your position at the negotiation table, allowing you to approach discussions with confidence and clarity.

- **Objectives:** During negotiations, my focus is on securing the best possible prices, favorable payment terms, and flexible delivery schedules. These elements are key to maintaining a smooth and cost-effective supply chain, particularly in the fast-paced restaurant industry.

- **Building Relationships:** Perhaps the most critical aspect of successful negotiations is relationship building. Developing strong, trusting relationships with suppliers not only makes negotiations smoother but also opens the door to more favorable terms, exclusive deals, and priority service during critical times. This relationship-driven approach has been a cornerstone of my strategy in every market I've worked in.

Payment Terms

Definition: Payment terms negotiation involves agreeing on the timing and methods of payment with suppliers, which can significantly impact cash flow management.

Introduction: In my experience, the way payment terms are negotiated can have a profound impact on a restaurant's financial health. Especially in new markets or during the early stages of a business, cash flow management becomes crucial. By securing favorable payment terms, I've been able to ensure that our outflows are well-aligned with our revenue cycles, which is essential for maintaining operational stability. Over the years, I've found that building a relationship of trust with suppliers often opens the door to more flexible and advantageous payment arrangements. Whether it's extending payment periods or securing discounts for early payments, effective negotiation of payment terms has always been a key strategy in managing the financial lifeblood of the operations I've overseen.

Techniques:

- **Negotiate Terms:** Engage with suppliers to establish payment terms that offer flexibility. Options such as extended payment periods or discounts for early payments can significantly ease cash flow pressures and provide financial breathing room during slower periods.

- **Financial Alignment:** Ensure that your payment schedules are synchronized with your business's revenue cycles. By aligning your financial obligations with your income streams, you can avoid cash crunches and maintain smooth financial operations.

- **Pay on Time:** Consistently paying on time strengthens your relationship with suppliers, building trust and potentially leading to better terms in the future. It also avoids late fees and maintains your reputation as a reliable partner.

- **Credit Limits:** It's crucial to stay within the credit limits set by your suppliers. Exceeding these limits can result in account blocking, disrupting the supply chain and potentially halting operations. Regularly monitor your credit usage to avoid such issues.

For example, in one of my operations, negotiating 60-day payment terms with key suppliers was instrumental in managing finances more effectively, allowing us to maintain liquidity during seasonal fluctuations.

Rebates on Purchases

Definition: Rebates on purchases involve negotiating with suppliers to receive monetary returns based on volume or value of purchases over a specific period.

Introduction: In my experience, leveraging rebates can be a highly effective strategy for enhancing profitability, especially in high-volume operations. When managing large-scale purchases, whether for a chain of restaurants or a single busy outlet, the cumulative savings from rebates can significantly reduce the net cost of goods. This approach not only helps in maintaining tight control over food costs but also allows for reinvestment in other critical areas of the business. By carefully tracking purchase volumes and ensuring that rebate agreements are properly executed, I've been able to turn these rebates into a reliable source of cost savings, contributing directly to the bottom line.

Techniques:

- **Negotiate Rebates:** Work with suppliers to arrange volume-based rebates that lower the overall cost of supplies. This can be particularly beneficial when you have consistent purchasing patterns or are able to consolidate orders across multiple locations.

- **Track and Claim:** Keep meticulous records of your purchases to meet the thresholds required for rebates. Ensure that all eligible rebates are claimed in a timely manner and applied to your accounts. This not only maximizes your savings but also reinforces the value of your supplier partnerships.

For example, in one operation, negotiating a 5% rebate on monthly purchases exceeding $10,000 provided substantial savings over the course of a year. By diligently tracking our purchasing data, we were able to consistently meet the threshold, resulting in a significant reduction in our overall food cost.

Alternative and Multiple Suppliers

In the restaurant industry, maintaining dish quality despite fluctuations in supply chains and market conditions is vital to operational success. One key strategy I've implemented across various operations is establishing relationships with alternative or multiple suppliers for the same ingredient. This approach ensures that even if one supplier experiences issues, the consistency and quality of your dishes remain unaffected.

For example, by using a generic ingredient name like "potatoes" in your recipes, such as those used for making French fries, you can switch between suppliers without needing to update the recipe or worry about fluctuating costs. The preparation method and quantity remain constant, allowing you to maintain a steady food cost and ensure that customers receive the same quality product every time, regardless of the source of the ingredients.

Having multiple suppliers not only provides flexibility but also strengthens your negotiating power, as it ensures you're not overly reliant on a single source. This strategy has proven invaluable in ensuring operational resilience and maintaining the high standards that customers expect, even in the face of supply chain disruptions.

Advantages of Multiple Suppliers

- **Price Flexibility:** Having multiple suppliers allows a restaurant to benefit from varying prices due to differences in sourcing, scale, and market conditions. This flexibility enables you to choose the most cost-effective option without compromising quality. By strategically selecting suppliers, you can better control food costs and buffer against price volatility, ensuring consistent profitability even in fluctuating markets.

- **Supply Reliability:** Relying on a single supplier for critical ingredients can be risky, as any disruption—such as crop failure, logistical issues, or supplier instability—could severely impact your operations. By diversifying your supplier base, you enhance the reliability of your supply chain, ensuring that your restaurant always has the necessary ingredients to meet demand, thereby preventing any interruptions in service.

- **Quality Assurance:** Engaging with multiple suppliers allows for ongoing comparison of ingredient quality. This competitive environment encourages suppliers to maintain high standards to secure and retain your business. As a result, your restaurant benefits from consistently high-quality ingredients, which translates to better customer satisfaction and a stronger brand reputation.

Implementation Strategy

1. **Ingredient Specification:** Clearly define the quality and specifications of ingredients in your purchasing contracts to ensure consistency across all suppliers. This includes details like size, ripeness, variety, and other relevant criteria that affect the ingredient's suitability for your recipes. By setting strict standards, you ensure that all suppliers deliver products that meet your restaurant's requirements.

2. **Supplier Evaluation:** Regularly evaluate suppliers based on criteria such as price, quality, reliability, and service. This ongoing assessment helps you make informed decisions about which suppliers to continue working with, allowing you to maintain a high standard of ingredients while optimizing costs.

3. **Price Negotiation:** Leverage the competition among multiple suppliers to negotiate better prices. However, it's crucial to ensure that cost savings do not lead to a compromise in ingredient quality. Striking a balance between cost-effectiveness and quality is key to maintaining the integrity of your menu.

4. **Communication and Feedback:** Maintain open lines of communication with all suppliers. Regularly provide feedback on the quality of ingredients and address any issues that arise. This dialogue fosters continuous improvement and helps suppliers better align with your restaurant's needs.

5. **Inventory Management:** Adapt your inventory management practices to efficiently handle multiple suppliers. This might involve updating how ingredients are tracked and stored to accommodate variations in packaging or

delivery schedules from different suppliers. Effective inventory management ensures that you can seamlessly integrate products from various sources without disrupting operations.

By adopting a strategy of having alternative or multiple suppliers for the same ingredient, restaurants can enhance operational resilience, maintain consistent quality in their offerings, and optimize food cost management effectively. This approach not only ensures a steady supply of high-quality ingredients but also provides flexibility in pricing, reducing the risk of disruptions and helping to maintain profitability in a competitive market.

Part Seven:

Sales and Revenue Management

Sales and Revenue Management

Sales and revenue management in the restaurant industry involves strategies to optimize pricing, maximize revenue, and ensure the profitability of menu items. Effective management includes understanding and applying various pricing techniques and monitoring sales performance to make informed business decisions.

Menu Pricing

Drawing from years of navigating the complex landscape of the hospitality industry, I've come to appreciate the art and science of menu pricing. This crucial aspect of restaurant management involves more than just covering costs—it requires a strategic alignment with market dynamics, customer expectations, and competitive positioning. In this section, we'll delve into how to set menu prices effectively, ensuring they not only reflect the value of the food and service offered but also contribute to the financial health and brand perception of your establishment. Through a blend of personal insights and industry best practices, we'll explore how to balance profitability with customer satisfaction in a competitive marketplace.

Introduction: Menu pricing involves setting prices that balance covering costs, generating profit, and meeting customer expectations. It requires analyzing market trends, customer preferences, and competitor pricing to ensure menu items are competitively priced.

Suggested Sample Analysis:

Trend	Description	Impact on Menu Pricing	Example Data (Hypothetical)
Plant-Based Dining	Increasing consumer preference for plant-based meals.	Higher prices for innovative plant-based dishes.	20% increase in plant-based menu items from 2022 to 2023.
Local and Organic Foods	Growing demand for locally sourced and organic ingredients.	Higher ingredient costs, leading to higher menu prices.	15% increase in menu prices for dishes with local ingredients.
Technology Integration	Increased use of online ordering and delivery services.	Additional costs for tech integration and delivery.	25% of total sales from online orders in 2023.
Health-Conscious Choices	Rising interest in health-conscious eating habits.	Higher prices for health-oriented menu options.	30% increase in sales of low-calorie menu items.
Economic Factors	Impact of inflation and economic conditions on dining out.	Adjustments in pricing to maintain profitability.	5% average increase in menu prices due to inflation in 2023.

This suggested data table shows how different trends can affect menu pricing strategies. For example, the increasing demand for plant-based dining options may require innovative ingredients and preparation methods, leading to higher prices. Similarly, sourcing local and organic foods can increase ingredient costs, which is reflected in the menu prices.

By staying informed about these trends and their impacts, restaurant managers can make strategic pricing decisions that align with market demands and maintain profitability.

Demand-Based Pricing:

Adjusting prices based on customer demand and perceived value.

Demand-based pricing is a strategic approach where prices are set primarily based on the consumer demand for a product or service rather than solely on the cost of production. This method involves adjusting prices according to the market conditions, consumer preferences, and perceived value. By closely monitoring market trends and consumer behavior, businesses can set prices that optimize their revenue and profitability.

For instance, during peak dining times or seasons with higher demand, restaurants can increase prices to maximize revenue. Conversely, during off-peak times, offering discounts or special deals can attract more customers and increase the capitation ratio, which is the proportion of actual sales to potential sales capacity. This dynamic pricing strategy helps in balancing supply and demand, ensuring that the restaurant remains competitive and appealing to its target market. Implementing demand-based pricing requires a deep understanding of market conditions and the ability to swiftly adjust pricing strategies to respond to changes in consumer demand effectively.

Competitive Pricing

Competitive pricing involves setting prices based on what competitors charge for similar dishes. This strategy helps in positioning the restaurant in the market and attracting customers while ensuring profitability.

How to do Competitive Pricing Analysis?

Conducting a competitive pricing analysis involves comparing similar offerings from different competitors to understand the market landscape and inform pricing strategies. Here's a table summarizing a competitive analysis of a popular dish, the grilled chicken salad, across five different restaurants:

Restaurant	Dish	Price	Portion Size	Portion Size	Quality	Additional Features	Customer Rating
Restaurant A	Grilled Chicken Salad	$12.99	300g	10.58 oz	High	Organic ingredients	4.5/5
Restaurant B	Grilled Chicken Salad	$10.50	280g	9.88 oz	Medium	Standard ingredients	4.0/5
Restaurant C	Grilled Chicken Salad	$14.00	350g	12.35 oz	Very High	Locally sourced, extra dressing	4.7/5
Restaurant D	Grilled Chicken Salad	$9.75	320g	11.29 oz	Medium	Includes breadsticks	3.8/5
Restaurant E	Grilled Chicken Salad	$13.50	300g	10.58 oz	High	Gluten-free option available	4.6/5

This table highlights various aspects such as price, portion size, quality, additional features, and customer ratings. By comparing these elements, restaurant managers can gain insights into how their pricing and offerings stack up against the competition. For instance, if **Restaurant A** wants to attract more customers, they might consider adding additional features or slightly adjusting their price to remain competitive with **Restaurant C**, which has a higher price but offers locally sourced ingredients and a higher customer rating.

Using such detailed analyses, restaurants can make informed decisions to fine-tune their pricing strategies, improve their offerings, and ultimately enhance their market position.

Pricing Techniques

Throughout my career, I have explored various pricing strategies to optimize profitability and competitiveness in the restaurant industry. In this section, we will delve into these strategies in detail, examining how they can be tailored to suit different types of menu items and dining experiences. This exploration will provide a comprehensive understanding of how effective pricing can significantly enhance a restaurant's financial performance.

Introduction: Pricing techniques involve methods and formulas used to set selling prices for menu items based on cost analysis, market demand, and profit margin goals. To maximize profitability while remaining competitive, restaurants must adopt strategic pricing techniques that reflect the cost of goods, market conditions, and customer expectations.

Ratios for Pricing Strategy

Ratios for pricing strategy refer to the mathematical formulas used to set menu prices based on the cost of goods sold (COGS) and desired profit margins. These ratios help you determine the selling price by considering both the direct costs associated with each item and the overall financial goals of your establishment. This approach ensures that prices are competitive yet sufficient to cover costs and achieve targeted profitability.

Here's a comprehensive approach to creating a pricing formula in a ratio style:

- **Food Cost Ratio:**

  Setting a desirable cost percentage then extracting the selling price.

  Assume the COGS for a dish is $4.00, and the desired food cost percentage is 25%.

  $$\text{Price} = \frac{\text{COGS}}{\text{Desired Food Cost Percentage}}$$

  $$\frac{\$4}{25\%} = \$16$$

  Therefore, the selling price should be $16 to achieve a 25% food cost percentage.

- **Profit Margin Ratio:**

  This ratio indicates the profitability of the menu item.

$$\text{Profit Margin} = \frac{(\text{Selling Price} - \text{COGS})}{\text{Selling Price}} \times 100$$

$$\frac{(\$16-\$4)}{\$16} \times 100 = 75\%$$

- **Contribution Margin Ratio:**

  This ratio shows the portion of sales that contributes to covering fixed costs and generating profit.

$$\text{Contribution Margin} = \frac{(\text{Selling Price} - \text{COGS})}{\text{Selling Price}}$$

$$\frac{(\$16-\$4)}{\$16} = 0.75$$

3. Markup Ratio:

This ratio helps determine the amount added to COGS to arrive at the selling price.

$$\text{Mark Up} = \frac{(\text{Selling Price} - \text{COGS})}{\text{COGS}} \times 100$$

$$\frac{(\$16-\$4)}{\$4} \times 100 = 300\%$$

Note: To effectively price menu items, consider using a ratio-based formula that accounts for the cost of goods sold (COGS) and desired profit margins. For instance, if the cost of a dish is $3.00 and you aim for a 25% food cost percentage, the selling price should be $12.00. This approach ensures profitability while maintaining competitive pricing.

Incorporate various ratios, such as profit margin, contribution margin, and markup, to refine your pricing strategy and ensure that each menu item contributes appropriately to your overall financial goals. For example, a grilled chicken salad with a COGS of $3.00 and a selling price of $12.00 results in a profit margin of 75%, a contribution margin of 0.75, and a markup of 300%.

By systematically applying these formulas and ratios, you can achieve a balanced pricing strategy that supports both profitability and customer satisfaction.

Product Management

In my career, navigating the intricacies of product management has been pivotal. This entails overseeing the lifecycle of menu items—from their inception and pricing strategy to garnering customer feedback and making necessary adjustments. This meticulous approach ensures each dish not only adheres to quality and cost specifications but also aligns with the restaurant's brand and customer expectations. Effective product management is crucial as it maximizes sales potential and heightens customer satisfaction by consistently offering products that resonate with our target audience.

Introduction: Product management in the context of a restaurant involves overseeing the entire lifecycle of menu items—from conception and pricing to customer feedback and adjustments. This strategic approach ensures that every dish not only meets the quality and cost standards but also aligns with the restaurant's brand and customer expectations. Effective product management maximizes sales potential and enhances customer satisfaction by consistently delivering products that resonate with the target market.

Positioning Quadrants

Definition: Positioning quadrants are a strategic tool used in product management to categorize menu items based on their popularity and profitability.

Introduction: This method helps you make informed decisions about which dishes to promote, revise, or remove from the menu, optimizing the overall menu performance.

Use positioning quadrants to analyze and optimize pricing and costing strategies based on your desired profitability and customer demand.

Techniques:

- **Quadrant Analysis:** Divide menu items into four quadrants based on popularity and profitability (e.g., Stars, Plow Horses, Puzzles, Dogs). Use this analysis to make informed decisions about pricing and menu placement.

- **Adjust Strategies:** For high-demand, low-profit items (Plow Horses), consider adjusting portion sizes or pricing to increase profitability. For low-demand, high-profit items (Puzzles), find ways to boost their appeal through marketing or repositioning.

- **Menu Design:** Design the menu to highlight high-profit, high-demand items (Stars). Use strategic placement and visual cues to draw attention to these items.

- **Regular Reviews:** Conduct regular reviews of the menu using the positioning quadrant analysis to ensure it remains balanced and profitable.

Low Risk & High-Risk Products

Definition: Low risk products are stable, dependable menu items that consistently contribute to a restaurant's profitability due to their steady demand and predictable costs. High-risk products, however, carry potential for higher rewards but are more volatile and uncertain, often influenced by fluctuating market trends, seasonal availability, or experimental flavors that may or may not resonate with customers.

Classify products based on risk factors such as perishability and cost to implement appropriate management strategies.

Techniques:

- **Classification:** Identify and classify products based on risk factors such as shelf life, cost, and demand. Use labels and color-coding to easily distinguish between high and low-risk items.

- **Inventory Management:** Implement stricter inventory controls for high-risk items, including more frequent stock counts and stricter FIFO (First In, First Out) practices. For low-risk items, maintain standard inventory practices.

- **Waste Reduction:** For high-risk, perishable items, closely monitor usage and adjust ordering quantities to minimize waste. Implement recipes and specials to use up excess stock before it expires.
- **Supplier Relationships:** Work with suppliers to ensure timely and reliable deliveries for high-risk items. Consider negotiating shorter lead times or smaller, more frequent deliveries to reduce holding costs.

Low Profitability & High Profitability Products

Definition: Low profitability products are items that yield lower margins compared to other menu options, often due to higher ingredient costs or lower customer demand. Conversely, high profitability products generate substantial margins, usually because of their popularity and the cost-effective nature of their ingredients, allowing for a greater markup while still attracting customer purchases.

Identify low and high profitability products to focus on promoting high-margin items.

Techniques:

- **Profit Analysis:** Conduct a profitability analysis of all menu items to identify high and low-margin products. Use this information to guide marketing and menu placement decisions.
- **Promotions:** Develop marketing strategies to promote high-profit items, such as special offers, upselling techniques, and prime menu placement.
- **Cost Control:** Review the cost structure of low-profit items and look for ways to reduce costs without compromising quality. This could include negotiating better prices with suppliers or adjusting portion sizes.
- **Menu Engineering:** Use menu engineering techniques to redesign the menu, emphasizing high-profit items and de-emphasizing or removing low-profit ones.

High Consumption Products and The Economies of Scale

Definition: High consumption products are items that sell in large volumes, often staples of the menu that consistently appeal to customers. The economies of scale refer to the cost advantages that businesses obtain due to the scale of operation, with cost per unit of output generally decreasing with increasing scale as fixed costs are spread out over more units of output.

Introduction: This principle applies to high consumption products as their bulk production and purchasing can significantly reduce their overall cost.

Leverage economies of scale for high consumption products to reduce costs and improve profitability.

Techniques:

- **Bulk Purchasing:** Identify high consumption products and negotiate bulk purchase agreements with suppliers to benefit from economies of scale. Ensure that storage capacity and shelf life are considered to avoid waste.

- **Standardization:** Standardize recipes and preparation methods for high consumption items to streamline operations and reduce variability. This helps in achieving consistent quality and controlling costs.

- **Usage Monitoring:** Implement systems to monitor the usage of high consumption products closely. Analyze data to predict future needs accurately and adjust purchasing accordingly.

- **Supplier Relationships:** Build strong relationships with suppliers to negotiate better terms and ensure a reliable supply of high consumption items. Consider consolidating orders to increase bargaining power.

Pricing an Online Menu

In my journey managing various digital food service platforms, I've learned that pricing an online menu requires careful consideration of unique factors that differ from traditional in-house menu pricing. This includes understanding online market competition, factoring in delivery costs, and recognizing the distinctive purchasing behaviors of customers on digital platforms. It's a balancing act to cover these added expenses while staying competitively priced in a market where customers can easily compare options. Emphasizing the necessity of strategizing prices effectively, this section explores how to optimize online sales and sustain profitability.

What to Consider

Here are some key considerations for pricing an online menu:

- When pricing an online menu, factor in additional costs such as delivery fees, packaging, and platform commissions.

- Adjust menu prices to cover these costs while remaining competitive.

- Regularly review and update online menu prices based on performance and feedback.

Menu Revenue and Updates

In my professional journey, ensuring the menu not only attracts customers but also drives revenue has been pivotal. Regular updates and revisions to the menu can reflect current market conditions, seasonal availability, and evolving customer preferences, all of which are crucial for maintaining and enhancing restaurant profitability.

Definition: Menu revenue refers to the income generated from the sales of menu items, while menu updates involve adjusting the menu's offerings to optimize financial performance and customer satisfaction.

Introduction: This process includes adding new dishes, removing underperforming items, and adjusting prices based on cost changes and competitive analysis.

Regularly review and update your menu to reflect changes in costs, market trends, and customer preferences.

Techniques:

- **Data Analysis:** Analyze sales data, customer feedback, and market trends to identify popular and underperforming items. Adjust the menu accordingly.

- **Cost Monitoring**: Regularly review ingredient costs and adjust menu prices to maintain profitability. Use a food cost percentage formula to determine appropriate pricing.

- **Seasonal Updates**: Update the menu seasonally to incorporate fresh, in-season ingredients, which are often cheaper and of higher quality.

- **Testing**: Introduce new items as specials to test customer response before making them permanent. Use customer feedback to refine recipes and pricing.

Dine In vs Take Away vs Online Ordering and Delivery

From my extensive experience in managing various restaurant formats, I've observed that the operational and financial dynamics significantly differ among dine-in, take-away, and online ordering systems. Understanding these distinctions is essential for optimizing each channel's revenue potential and ensuring customer satisfaction across all service modes.

This section explores the distinct aspects of dine-in, take-away, and online ordering and delivery services in a restaurant setting. Each service mode has unique operational requirements and contributes differently to a restaurant's revenue and customer experience.

Consider different cost structures and pricing strategies for dine-in, take-away, and delivery services.

Techniques:

- **Cost Analysis**: Calculate the different cost structures for dine-in, take-away, and delivery, including packaging, delivery fees, and service charges. Adjust pricing strategies accordingly to cover these additional costs.

- **Menu Adjustments**: Offer a streamlined menu for take-away and delivery, focusing on items that travel well and maintain quality. Ensure pricing reflects the added convenience.

- **Promotion:** Use targeted promotions for each service type. For example, offer discounts on take-away orders during off-peak hours to boost sales.
- **Technology:** Invest in reliable online ordering systems and partner with delivery platforms to ensure a smooth customer experience. Monitor online reviews and feedback to make improvements.

Sales Strategy by Channel

Drawing from my own journey in the food and beverage industry, I've learned that a nuanced approach to sales strategies can significantly enhance performance across different service channels. Each channel offers unique opportunities and challenges that require tailored strategies to maximize revenue and customer engagement.

This section delves into the specific sales strategies appropriate for various service channels within a restaurant context, such as dine-in, take-away, and online ordering. It discusses how to effectively align marketing, pricing, and service delivery strategies with the operational characteristics and customer expectations of each channel.

Developing strategies for different sales channels, considering cost implications and customer preferences.

Techniques:

- **Cost Structure Analysis:** Analyze the cost structures for dine-in, take-away, and delivery services. Consider factors such as packaging, delivery fees, and service charges. Adjust pricing strategies to cover these costs and remain competitive.
- **Menu Customization:** Customize the menu for each sales channel to optimize preparation and maintain quality. For example, offer items that travel well for delivery and take-away, and create exclusive dine-in specials to enhance the in-house experience.
- **Promotions and Marketing:** Develop targeted promotions for each sales channel. Use data and customer feedback to create effective marketing strategies that cater to different preferences and behaviors.

- **Technology Integration:** Invest in reliable online ordering systems and partner with delivery platforms to streamline the customer experience. Ensure that your technology infrastructure supports efficient order processing and accurate tracking.

- **Customer Feedback:** Regularly collect and analyze customer feedback for each sales channel. Use this data to make informed decisions about menu adjustments, pricing strategies, and service improvements.

Promotions and Their Impact on Cost

I've seen firsthand how promotions can serve as a double-edged sword. While they are powerful tools for boosting traffic and sales, their impact on the bottom line must be judiciously managed to avoid any adverse effects on profitability.

Promotions can drive customer traffic and increase sales, but they must be managed carefully to avoid negatively impacting profitability.

This section explores the strategic use of promotions in the restaurant business, emphasizing the need for careful planning and execution to enhance profitability without compromising financial health.

Techniques:

- **Setting Clear Objectives:** Clearly define what you aim to achieve with each promotion, be it attracting new customers, enhancing brand visibility, or increasing sales during slower periods. This focus will guide all other decisions related to the promotion.

- **Cost Analysis:** Evaluate all costs associated with the promotion, including reduced pricing, marketing materials, and any additional staff required. This analysis will help determine if the potential revenue increase justifies the expense.

- **Break-Even Analysis:** Use break-even analysis to pinpoint the volume of sales needed to cover the costs of the promotion. This critical assessment aids in setting realistic and achievable sales goals.

- **Strategic Discounting:** Opt for discounts on higher-margin items or bundle them to maintain or increase the profit margin. This tactic helps in leveraging promotions to improve profitability rather than just boosting sales volume.

- **Monitoring and Adjusting:** Implement systems to monitor the performance of promotions in real-time. Adapt your strategy based on actual sales data to optimize outcomes and mitigate any potential negative impacts.

- **Customer Feedback:** Solicit and analyze customer feedback regarding the promotion. Insights gathered can be invaluable in refining future promotional strategies and tailoring offers to better meet customer expectations and business objectives.

Part Eight:
Financial Planning

Financial Planning

In the world of business, particularly in the food and beverage industry, financial planning is a multifaceted process that requires a strategic and flexible approach. Whether you're launching a new venture or managing an established restaurant, effective financial planning is the key to maintaining profitability and growth. Through my career experience, I've identified and applied various financial models, each serving distinct purposes depending on the business context.

In this guide, we'll explore several critical methods of financial planning, each one provides unique benefits and challenges, but understanding how and when to apply these strategies ensures that all aspects of financial planning are covered. By diving into each approach, we will uncover the best-use scenarios for businesses at various stages, whether they are startups, expansions, or mature operations. The ultimate goal is to create a financial plan that aligns with your business model, operational efficiency, and market conditions while maintaining a clear path to profitability.

Reverse Engineer Your Financials

Definition: Reverse engineering your numbers is a strategic approach to financial planning that begins with identifying your desired net profit and working backwards to determine the appropriate selling prices and corresponding food costs.

Introduction: This method involves calculating all associated costs on your profit and loss (P&L) statement and integrating sales forecasts with multiple scenarios to ensure you meet your financial goals.

Step-by-Step Strategy:

1. **Determine Desired Net Profit:** Start by defining your target net profit. This is the amount you aim to retain after all expenses are paid. For example, if you want a net profit of $100,000 annually, this becomes your starting point.

2. **Identify Fixed and Variable Costs:** List all your fixed costs (rent, salaries, utilities) and variable costs (maintenance, marketing, G&A). Let's assume your fixed costs amount to $200,000 annually, and variable costs are $75,000.

3. **Calculate Total Costs:** Add your fixed and variable costs to determine total expenses. In this case:

   Total Costs = Fixed Costs + Variable

   Costs = $200,000 + $75,000 = $275,000

4. **Incorporate Desired Net Profit:** Add your desired net profit to your total costs to find the required revenue before incorporating food cost:

   Revenue Before Food Cost = Total Costs + Desired Net Profit

   $270,000 + $100,000 = $375,000

5. **Required Revenue:** We will consider the food cost fixed at 25% of revenue, 75% of the revenue must cover your fixed costs, non-food variable costs, and profit:

   75% x Revenue = $375,000

   $$\text{Revenue} = \frac{375{,}000}{75\%} = \$500{,}000$$

6. **Estimate Sales Forecast:** Develop sales forecasts for three scenarios: Worst Case, Mid Case, and Best Case.

   - **Worst Case:** Assume low customer turnout, resulting in lower revenue.
   - **Mid Case:** Assume average customer turnout, resulting in moderate revenue.
   - **Best Case:** Assume high customer turnout, resulting in maximum revenue.

   For simplicity, let's assume the following annual number of guests for each scenario:

   - **Worst Case:** 15,000 customer turnouts.
   - **Mid Case:** 18,000 customer turnouts.
   - **Best Case:** 20,000 customer turnouts.

7. **Determine Required Selling Prices:** Calculate the average required selling price per unit (e.g., per dish) for each scenario by dividing the required revenue by the number of expected sales.

   Required Selling Price = Number of Dishes / Required Revenue

   For each scenario:

   - **Worst Case:** $500,000 / 15,000 = $33.33 Selling price per dish
   - **Mid Case:** $500,000 / 18,000 = $27.78 Selling price per dish
   - **Best Case:** $500,000 / 20,000 = $25 Selling price per dish

By reverse engineering your numbers, you establish a clear pathway from your desired net profit to your required selling prices.

This method ensures that all expenses are accounted for and adjust your pricing strategy based on realistic sales forecasts.

Note: The selling price must align with the market competition. If the market is against your pricing strategy, then you should consider adjustments to your costs, or some compromise on your desired net profit.

Evaluating worst-case, mid-case, and best-case scenarios allows you to remain flexible and responsive to market conditions, ultimately supporting the financial health and profitability of your restaurant.

Conclusion: Naturally, in an ideal world, the cost of ingredients for each dish remains relatively fixed, regardless of the number of dishes sold. This means that while the food cost percentage might adjust in each scenario, the actual cost of ingredients per dish would not change. In higher sales scenarios, the **food cost percentage effectively drops**, as the fixed ingredient costs are spread over a greater number of units. This is the core purpose of the **reverse engineering** approach: it allows you to work backwards from your financial goals to ensure that the selling price, cost structure, and projected sales all align. By playing around with the numbers, you can ensure that your financial statement makes sense and fits within the competitive market. If the final calculations don't allow for profitability at a marketable price, it's a clear indication that the project may not be feasible, signaling a no-go decision.

Allocating a Budget form Forecasted Sales

Definition: Allocating a budget from forecasted sales is a strategic approach particularly useful for existing businesses. This method involves distributing your forecasted sales revenue across various expense categories, ensuring each category is adequately funded while maintaining a desired net profit margin.

Introduction: This approach allows you to determine an appropriate budget for food costs, which in turn helps set realistic selling prices that align with market conditions and competition.

Step-by-Step Strategy:

1. **Forecast Sales Revenue:** Start by projecting your sales revenue based on historical data and market trends. For example, assume your forecasted annual sales revenue is $1,000,000.

2. **Allocate Percentages for Fixed Expenses:** Distribute your forecasted sales revenue among various fixed expenses. Typical allocations might be:

   - **Rent: 20%**
   - **Payroll: 18%**
   - **Marketing: 3%**
   - **Other expenses** (utilities, insurance, etc.): **9%**

   Calculate the budget for each category:

   - **Rent:** 20% x $1,000,000 = $200,000
   - **Payroll:** 18% x $1,000,000 = $180,000
   - **Other Expenses:** 9% x $1,000,000 = $90,000
   - **Marketing:** 3% x $1,000,000 = $30,000

3. **Determine Desired Net Profit:** Set your target net profit margin.

   For example, if you aim for a 20% net profit:

   - **Desired Net Profit:** 20% x $1,000,000 = $200,000

4. **Calculate Remaining Budget for Variable Costs:** Subtract the allocated fixed expenses and desired net profit from the forecasted sales revenue to find the remaining budget for variable costs, including food costs:

- **Remaining Budget:**

  Revenue – Net Profit – Rent – Payroll – Other Expenses – Marketing = Remaining Budget

  $1,000,000 - $200,000 - $200,000 - $180,000 - $90,000 - $30,000 = $300,000

5. **Allocate Budget for Food Costs:** The remaining budget typically includes food costs and other related variable expenses. If you aim for a food cost percentage that allows for competitive pricing, market alignment and the restaurant's operational efficiency, you might allocate the total remaining budget:

   300,000 / 1,000,000 = 30%

6. **Set Selling Prices:** Based on the allocated food cost budget, determine the average cost per dish and set selling prices accordingly. If your food cost should be 30% of the selling price, reverse calculate the necessary selling price:

   Selling Price = Food Cost / 30%

   If we consider $6.75 the cost of the dish

   $6.75 / 30% = $22.5 Selling Price

7. **Market and Competition Considerations:** Assess the market and competition to ensure your prices are competitive. If the calculated price is too high, adjustments to the allocations may be necessary to achieve a feasible selling price while maintaining profitability.

8. **Fine-Tuning Allocations:** If the selling price does not align with market conditions, revisit your expense allocations. Adjust categories such as marketing or payroll slightly to find a balance that allows for competitive pricing and desired profit margins.

   By allocating a budget from forecasted sales, you can strategically manage expenses while aiming for a desired net profit. This method helps in setting realistic food cost budgets and selling prices, ensuring they are competitive and sustainable. Regularly reviewing and fine-tuning these allocations based on market conditions will help maintain a winning business proposition.

Understanding Average Check and Sales Mix

Definition: Understanding the average check and sales mix involves analyzing the average amount spent per customer and the distribution of sales across different menu items. This analysis helps you identify which items are driving revenue and how customer choices impact overall profitability.

Introduction: I've learned the significant role that understanding the average check and sales mix plays in shaping restaurant profitability. This knowledge not only helped me in setting realistic expectations but also in fine-tuning the menu to meet customer preferences and maximize revenue, in every business I led.

The Reality

Restaurants rarely sell just one item. Instead, they offer a variety of menu items, each contributing to the overall revenue. The concept of the **average check** (or average ticket) and **sales mix** is crucial for understanding how different items combine to influence total sales and profitability. This knowledge helps in making informed decisions about menu pricing, promotions, and marketing strategies to achieve financial goals.

Average Check:

The average check is the average amount of money a customer spends per visit. It is calculated by dividing the total revenue by the number of customers or checks. For instance, if your restaurant generates $10,000 from 500 checks, the average check is:

- **Average Check:** $10,000 / 500 = $20

Sales Mix:

The sales mix refers to the combination and proportion of different items sold.

Understanding the sales mix is essential because different items have different cost structures and profit margins. For example, beverages typically have higher margins than main courses.

Building the Average Check through Sales Mix:

Consider how different courses contribute to the average check. A typical meal might include multiple courses, such as appetizers, main courses, desserts, and beverages. Here's how a sample sales mix could look:

- **Appetizer: $7**
- **Main Course: $18**
- **Desserts: $8**
- **Beverages: $6**

- For a **3-course meal** (appetizer, main course, and beverage):
  Average Check: $7 + $18 + $6 = $31

- For a **4-course meal** (appetizer, main course, dessert, and beverage):
  Average Check: $7 + $18 + $8 + $6 = $39

- For a **5-course meal** (2x appetizers, main course, dessert, and beverage):
  Average Check: $7 + $7 + $18 + $8 + $6 = $46

Strategic Application:

By analyzing the average check and sales mix, you can make strategic decisions to optimize profitability.

1. **Menu Engineering:** The strategic design and layout of a menu to influence customer choices, maximize profitability, and enhance the dining experience by offering set menus and promotions that align with consumer preferences and cost structures.

   - **Combos and Set Menus:** Create set menus or combos that encourage customers to purchase multiple courses, thereby increasing the average check.

   - **Promotions:** Offer promotions on high-margin items to boost profitability.

2. **Sales Forecasting:** The process of predicting future sales using historical data, considering factors like sales trends and market conditions, to make informed decisions about inventory, staffing, and marketing.

   - **Sales Mix Analysis:** Analyze historical sales data to determine the most popular items and their contribution to revenue. This helps in forecasting sales and planning inventory.

   - **Scenario Planning:** Develop multiple scenarios (e.g., worst case, mid case, best case) to understand the impact of different sales mixes on revenue and profit.

3. **Marketing Strategies:** Tactics used to promote and sell products by targeting specific customer segments and optimizing promotional efforts to increase visibility and drive sales of high-margin items.

   - **Targeted Promotions:** Use the sales mix data to design targeted promotions that drive sales of high-margin items.

   - **Customer Segmentation:** Segment customers based on their purchasing behavior and tailor marketing efforts to different segments.

4. **Operational Adjustments:** Modifications made in day-to-day operations, including staff training and inventory management, to improve efficiency, reduce costs, and enhance customer service by aligning with sales and marketing strategies.

   - **Staff Training:** Train staff to upsell and promote high-margin items.

   - **Inventory Management:** Adjust inventory based on sales mix trends to minimize waste and reduce costs.

Understanding the average check and sales mix is essential for effective financial planning in the restaurant industry. By analyzing how different items contribute to total sales, you can make informed decisions about menu pricing, promotions, and marketing strategies. This approach helps you optimize revenue, manage costs, and achieve desired financial outcomes.

Capitation Ratio and Its Impact on Sales Mix

"Among the many metrics used to refine restaurant operations, the capitation ratio stands out as a particularly powerful tool, one that I have championed and implemented across numerous venues with remarkable success.

This ratio offers profound insights into customer behavior by quantifying the likelihood of menu selections. It is especially crucial for establishments like a la carte restaurants and quick-service restaurants, where the menu variety is vast, and each choice influences the financial outcome.

My experience has proven that mastering the capitation ratio can transform an establishment's strategic approach to menu design and customer engagement, ensuring that each item on the menu not only meets customer expectations but also contributes optimally to the establishment's profitability."

The capitation ratio measures the likelihood of each customer ordering a specific course, category, or item off the menu. This metric is particularly valuable for food and beverage (F&B) establishments that do not have a set menu, such as a la carte restaurants or quick-service restaurants (QSRs). Understanding the capitation ratio helps in determining the sales mix and, subsequently, affects the average check since each menu item has a different price.

For example, in a coffee shop, it is highly likely that nearly every customer will order a coffee, while only a smaller percentage will order food.

This can be represented as:

- 90% of customers order coffee
- 20% of customers order food

In a fine dining restaurant, the capitation ratio might look like this:

- 100% of customers order a main course
- 80% order an appetizer
- 40% order desserts
- 100% order beverages

- 20% order a hot beverage such as coffee

These ratios are crucial in understanding the sales mix. Since different courses, dishes, and items on the menu have varying prices, the capitation ratio directly impacts the average check.

As time progresses, this information is recorded in the restaurant operating system (ROS), and the capitation ratio becomes more accurate. Advanced ROS solutions use AI learning to analyze historical data and predict future patterns, allowing for better forecasting and strategic planning. This enables restaurants to optimize their menu offerings, pricing strategies, and marketing efforts to maximize profitability and customer satisfaction.

Determine Your Food Cost

Definition: Food cost determination is the process of calculating the total cost of ingredients used in each dish to ascertain the cost-effectiveness and profitability of menu items.

Introduction: This fundamental task not only impacts your pricing strategies but also influences menu planning and inventory control. As someone deeply invested in the meticulous management of food service operations, I have consistently utilized and refined food cost calculations to ensure each menu item not only delights the palate but also delivers on profitability.

Techniques:

- **Cost Calculation:** Begin by summing the cost of all ingredients for each dish to understand its direct expense.

- **Regular Updates:** Adjust these calculations as supplier prices fluctuate to maintain accuracy in your costing.

- **Automation via Software:** Implement recipe costing software to streamline the process, reducing manual errors and providing real-time food cost percentages.

For example, if a dish uses $6 worth of ingredients and sells for $24, the food cost percentage is 25%.

This metric is crucial for adjusting pricing strategies to ensure both competitiveness in the market and desired profit margins.

Dividing and Anticipating Your Overall Net Profit

Definition: Dividing and anticipating net profit involves the strategic forecasting of profits based on historical sales data, cost management, and budgeting to ensure financial goals are met.

Introduction: Understanding and anticipating your overall net profit is vital for long-term business sustainability. By consistently analyzing past performance and forecasting future profits, you can make informed decisions that guide your pricing strategies and cost management practices. This proactive approach allows you to stay ahead of potential financial challenges and ensure that your business continues to grow and thrive.

Techniques:

- **Forecasting Net Profit:** Use historical data to project future sales and costs, giving you a clear picture of anticipated profits.

- **Budget Creation:** Develop detailed budgets that outline expected revenues and expenses, providing a roadmap for achieving your financial goals.

- **Performance Monitoring:** Regularly compare your actual performance against these budgets to identify variances and take corrective action as needed.

- **Strategic Adjustments:** Use insights from your profit analysis to adjust pricing, streamline operations, and enhance cost management strategies, ensuring you stay on track to meet your desired profit margins.

Discounts

When offering discounts in restaurants, it is essential to understand their impact on revenue and food cost, and consequently, the bottom line. Discounts directly reduce the revenue generated from each sale, thereby affecting the overall profitability of the business.

Food cost percentages are typically calculated based on the full price of a dish. For example, if a dish is priced at $20 and the cost of ingredients is $6, the food cost percentage is 30%. However, when a discount is applied, the revenue from that dish decreases, but the cost of ingredients remains the same. This imbalance causes an increase in the food cost percentage.

To illustrate, consider a 20% discount on the $20 dish, reducing the sale price to $16. The food cost of $6 now represents 37.5% of the discounted price, a significant increase from the original 30%. This higher food cost percentage impacts the restaurant's margin and overall profitability.

When planning for discounts, it is crucial to adjust budgets and projections accordingly. Calculate the new food cost percentage based on the discounted prices and assess the impact on your profit margins. For instance, if you know that you will offer discounts regularly, you can plan for a higher food cost percentage in your budget and make necessary adjustments in other areas to maintain desired profit margins.

Example:

- Original Dish Price: $20
- Original Food Cost: $6 (30% Food Cost)

With a 20% discount:

- Discounted Price: $16
- Food Cost: $6 (37.5% Food Cost)

The increase in the food cost percentage must be accounted for in financial planning to ensure that the restaurant remains profitable even when discounts are applied. By carefully analyzing the impact of discounts on food cost and overall margins, restaurant managers can make informed decisions that balance attracting customers with maintaining profitability.

Other Items to Consider

Amortization of Small Wares and Guest Supplies

Definition: Amortization of small wares and guest supplies involves spreading the cost of these items over their useful life to manage expenses more effectively and avoid sudden financial strain.

Introduction: In restaurant operations, managing the cost of small wares and guest supplies can significantly impact cash flow. By amortizing these expenses, you can allocate the cost over the items' useful lifespan, ensuring that your financial statements reflect a more accurate picture of operational costs. This approach also aids in budgeting and planning for the eventual replacement of these items, allowing for smoother financial management.

Amortizing the cost of small wares and guest supplies helps spread expenses over their useful life, reducing the impact on cash flow. Let's take a look at some techniques.

Techniques:

- **Identify Amortizable Items:** Begin by identifying which small wares (e.g., utensils, cookware) and guest supplies (e.g., linens, toiletries) can be amortized. Consider the lifespan and cost of each item to determine whether amortization is appropriate.

- **Calculate Depreciation:**

  - **Straight-Line Method:** Apply the straight-line depreciation method to evenly distribute the cost over the item's useful life. For instance, if a piece of equipment costs $1,000 and has a lifespan of 5 years, you would depreciate it at $200 per year.

  - **Recording Depreciation:** Ensure that depreciation expenses are accurately recorded in your accounting system. This practice will provide a clear view of the true cost of operations over time and help in making informed financial decisions.

- **Budgeting:**
  - **Incorporate Depreciation:** Include depreciation expenses in your budget to account for the gradual wear and tear of small wares and guest supplies, ensuring that these costs are anticipated and managed effectively.
  - **Replacement Planning:** Strategically plan for the replacement of items before they reach the end of their useful life. This proactive approach prevents operational disruptions and supports smoother financial planning, ensuring that you have the necessary resources to replace essential items when needed.

Part Nine:
Using Technology

Using Technology

Throughout my career in the restaurant industry, I've had the opportunity to work with more than a dozen different technology systems, each bringing its own set of strengths and challenges. As someone deeply involved in the operational side of restaurants, I've seen firsthand how the right technology can transform a business, turning chaotic operations into a well-oiled machine.

My journey has also led me to become an advisor, subject matter expert, and product owner for a tech company that specializes in developing Restaurant Operating Systems (ROS). This role has given me a unique perspective on how crucial these systems are in driving efficiency, reducing costs, and ultimately boosting profitability in the restaurant world. I'm passionate about leveraging technology to make the complex simple and to help restaurateurs focus on what they do best—providing exceptional experiences for their customers.

In the following sections, I will guide you through the key aspects of using technology in restaurants, highlighting what to look for when choosing the right systems to support and enhance your operations.

ROS, IMS, and POS

In the modern restaurant industry, technology plays a crucial role in streamlining operations and enhancing efficiency. Restaurant Operating Systems (ROS), Inventory Management Systems (IMS), and Point of Sale (POS) systems are the backbone of this digital transformation. Together, they provide a seamless integration of front and back-of-house operations, ensuring that everything from managing inventory to processing customer orders runs smoothly.

With extensive experience in implementing and advising on these systems, I've seen firsthand how they can revolutionize restaurant management by providing real-time data, reducing errors, and ultimately driving profitability. In this section, I'll take you through the essential aspects of each system, helping you understand their importance and how to leverage them effectively in your restaurant. Here's how to choose and implement these systems:

Inventory Management Systems:

An Inventory Management System (IMS) is a software tool used to track and manage inventory levels, orders, sales, and deliveries within a restaurant. It helps ensure that the restaurant maintains optimal stock levels, minimizes waste, and prevents over-ordering. An IMS is essential for maintaining accurate inventory records and ensuring that ingredients are available when needed.

- **Quality System**: Ensure that high-quality inventory management software is used to track every item from purchase to sale. This minimizes waste and theft.

- **Best Fit for Your Operation**: Evaluate different systems based on your business size, menu complexity, and volume. Look for features such as real-time tracking, automated reordering, and integration with other systems.

- **Implementation**: Train staff on how to use the system effectively. Regularly update inventory data to maintain accuracy.

Point of Sale (POS) Systems:

A Point of Sale (POS) system is the technology used at the checkout point in a restaurant where customers make payments for their orders. Beyond processing transactions, modern POS systems also handle various functions such as tracking sales data, managing customer orders, and integrating with other systems like ROS and IMS for a seamless operational flow.

- **Importance**: A good POS system streamlines transactions, tracks sales data, and integrates with other systems for comprehensive business management.

- **Options and Selection**: Compare different POS systems based on ease of use, features, customer support, and cost. Consider options that offer mobile and online ordering capabilities.

- **Gold In, Gold Out:** Maintain the integrity of your POS system by ensuring all transactions are accurately recorded and reconciled with inventory data.

Restaurant Operating Systems:

A Restaurant Operating System (ROS) is an integrated platform that combines various operational aspects of a restaurant, such as order management, inventory tracking, and employee scheduling, into one cohesive system. It serves as the central hub for managing all day-to-day activities, ensuring that different departments within the restaurant communicate effectively and operate efficiently.

- **Advanced Stage:** A Restaurant Operating System (ROS) is a comprehensive software platform designed to streamline and integrate various operational aspects of a restaurant. By combining features of point-of-sale (POS) systems with inventory management solutions, ROS provides a unified approach to managing a restaurant's front and back-end processes.

- **Larger Businesses:** With capabilities to oversee production stations, manage inventory and suppliers, and handle multi-unit operations, a ROS helps restaurants reduce waste, optimize staffing, and improve overall operational accuracy.

- **Centralized:** Such a system enhances efficiency by offering functionalities such as real-time data analysis, recipe management, expiry tracking, and customizable reporting. By centralizing and automating key processes, enables managers to focus more on delivering exceptional customer service and strategic growth.

Mapping an IMS with an ERP System

Definition: Mapping an Inventory Management System (IMS) with an Enterprise Resource Planning (ERP) system involves integrating these two systems to ensure seamless data flow and coordination between inventory management and broader business operations. This integration enables real-time visibility and accuracy across inventory, procurement, sales, and financial data.

Introduction: Integrating your IMS with an ERP system is a strategic move that can significantly enhance your restaurant's operational efficiency. Throughout my career, I've seen firsthand how this integration can eliminate redundancies, streamline workflows, and provide critical insights that drive better decision-making. By mapping your IMS to an ERP system, you not only gain a more comprehensive view of your inventory but also align it with the larger goals of your business, from procurement to financial reporting. In the following section, I'll guide you through the key aspects of this integration and what to consider in making the most out of these powerful tools.

Integrate your IMS with an ERP to streamline your operations and obtain accurate data.

Techniques:

- **Integration Plan:** Develop a detailed integration plan that outlines the steps, timeline, and resources required for integrating the IMS with the ERP system.

- **Data Mapping:** Map the data fields between the IMS and ERP systems to ensure accurate data transfer. This includes inventory levels, purchase orders, and financial records.

- **Testing:** Conduct thorough testing to identify and resolve any issues before going live. Involve key stakeholders in the testing process to ensure all requirements are met.

- **Training:** Train staff on how to use the integrated systems effectively. Provide documentation and support to ensure a smooth transition.

- **Monitoring:** Regularly monitor the performance of the integrated systems and address any issues promptly to maintain data accuracy and operational efficiency.

Centralizing IMS System Accessibility

Definition: Centralizing IMS access refers to the practice of consolidating control over who can access and modify the Inventory Management System (IMS) within a restaurant operation. This approach limits administrative permissions to key personnel, ensuring that only authorized users can make changes to inventory data, thereby enhancing security, data accuracy, and operational efficiency.

Introduction: Centralizing IMS access is not just about improving efficiency—it's about safeguarding your restaurant's data integrity and maintaining control over inventory management. By ensuring that only authorized personnel can make changes, you prevent unauthorized access and reduce the risk of errors that could disrupt operations. Limited admin access allows you to maintain a tight grip on who can alter crucial data, ensuring that every modification is intentional and properly vetted. In this section, we'll delve into the strategies for implementing centralized IMS access and the benefits of maintaining strict control over your inventory systems.

Centralize IMS access to prevent unauthorized changes and ensure data integrity, with limited admin access to maintain control.

Techniques:

- **Access Control:** Implement strict access controls for the IMS, granting admin privileges only to authorized personnel. Use role-based access to limit user permissions based on their responsibilities.

- **Centralized Management:** Centralize the management of the IMS to ensure consistent policies and procedures are followed. Designate a system administrator to oversee access and monitor system activity.

- **Audit Trails:** Enable audit trails to track changes made to the IMS. Regularly review these logs to identify and address any unauthorized access or changes.

- **Training:** Train users on the importance of data integrity and the proper use of the IMS. Emphasize the need for following established procedures and protocols.

- **Regular Reviews:** Conduct regular reviews of user access and permissions to ensure they are appropriate and up to date. Adjust access levels as needed based on changes in roles and responsibilities.

System Reports and Business Analysis

Definition: System reports and business analysis involve the extraction and interpretation of data from restaurant management systems to track performance metrics and make informed operational and financial decisions.

Introduction: Accurate and timely reporting is the backbone of any successful restaurant business. Throughout my career, I've had the opportunity to work with a multitude of systems and reports, each offering unique insights into the inner workings of the business. I've learned that data, when harnessed correctly, is one of the most powerful tools at your disposal. It's not just about numbers; it's about understanding the story they tell and using that story to steer your business toward success. In this section, I'll share with you the essential reports that have been invaluable to me, how you can make data-driven decisions that truly impact your bottom line, and why managing sales tax accurately is critical to your financial health. These are the tools and techniques that have helped me stay ahead in the industry, and I'm confident they'll do the same for you.

Accurate reporting from your systems is essential for analyzing business performance and making informed decisions.

Techniques:

Essential Reports:

Definition: Essential reports are the key financial and operational data summaries that provide insights into sales, inventory, labor, and overall profitability, which are critical for daily decision-making.

Introduction: Understanding the various types of reports that your system can generate is fundamental to managing a successful restaurant. These reports not only help track sales and inventory but also provide a snapshot of your financial performance. Here's a breakdown of the essential reports you should be using:

Techniques:

- **Sales Reports:** Track daily, weekly, and monthly sales to identify trends and peak periods. Analyze sales by item, category, and time of day.

- **Inventory Reports:** Monitor stock levels, turnover rates, and waste to optimize inventory management. Identify slow-moving and fast-moving items.

- **Cost of Goods Sold (COGS) Reports:** Analyze COGS to manage expenses and improve profitability. Break down COGS by category for detailed insights.

- **Labor Reports:** Track labor costs and productivity. Compare labor expenses against sales to ensure efficient staffing.

- **Profit and Loss Statements:** Regularly review P&L statements to assess overall financial health. Identify areas for cost reduction and revenue enhancement.

Data-Driven Decisions:

Definition: Data-driven decisions involve making business choices based on actionable insights derived from the analysis of system-generated reports.

Introduction: Harnessing the power of data can transform your decision-making process. It's not just about having the data but understanding it and acting on it. Here's how you can use your system reports to drive your business forward:

Techniques:

- **Identify Trends:** Use reports to identify sales trends, customer preferences, and seasonal variations. Adjust menus and marketing strategies accordingly.

- **Performance Monitoring:** Monitor key performance indicators (KPIs) such as average ticket size, table turnover rate, and customer satisfaction scores.

- **Action Plans:** Develop action plans based on report findings. For example, if inventory reports show high waste, implement stricter portion control measures.

Understanding the Impact of Sales Tax on Reports

Understanding the impact of sales tax on reports involves separating taxes from sales figures to accurately assess business performance and make informed financial decisions.

One often overlooked aspect of financial reporting is the treatment of sales tax. In my experience, separating taxes from your sales figures is essential to understanding your true financial performance. Here's why and how to handle taxes correctly in your reports:

1. **Net Sales or Revenue Reporting**
   - **Why:** Including taxes in sales reports can distort financial metrics, particularly food cost percentages, and lead to false conclusions about your business's performance.
   - **How:** Ensure that your sales reports reflect net sales or revenue, which is the total sales amount excluding taxes. This provides a clearer picture of actual sales performance and profitability.

2. **Impact on Food Cost Calculations**
   - **Why:** Including taxes in sales figures can decrease your food cost percentage, making it appear that your food costs are lower than they actually are.
   - **How:** Calculate food costs based on net sales, ensuring that taxes are excluded. This way, you get an accurate measure of the cost of goods sold relative to the actual revenue generated from food and beverage sales.

3. **Legal Requirements and Inclusive Pricing**
   - **Why:** In some countries, businesses are required to include taxes like VAT (Value Added Tax) or GST (Goods and Services Tax) in the displayed prices of their products.
   - **How:** Even if taxes are included in the pricing for customers, ensure that your internal financial reports separate these taxes. Report prices exclusive of

taxes in your internal systems to maintain accurate food cost and profitability metrics.

4. **Taxes in the P&L Statement**

- **Why:** Taxes should be reported in the Profit and Loss (P&L) statement as a separate line item. This allows for clear visibility of the business's tax liabilities and ensures that all financial analysis is based on net figures.

- **How:** Structure your P&L to include a section for taxes, distinct from sales revenue and cost of goods sold. This helps in maintaining clarity and accuracy in financial reporting and analysis.

5. **Planning Recipes, Food Costs, and Raw Pricing**

- **Why:** When planning recipes and setting prices, it's important to base calculations on the actual cost of ingredients and preparation, not inflated by tax amounts.

- **How:** Use net selling prices (excluding taxes) when determining food costs, setting menu prices, and planning raw ingredient purchases. This ensures that your pricing strategy accurately reflects the true cost and desired profit margins.

By separating sales taxes from your sales reports and including them in your P&L statement, you ensure accurate financial tracking and better decision-making. This clarity allows for more precise food cost management, pricing strategies, and overall financial planning, leading to a more profitable and well-managed restaurant business.

Choosing the Right ROS

Selecting the right Restaurant Operating System (ROS) is one of the most critical decisions you'll make as a restaurateur. Over the years, I've navigated through a myriad of systems, each promising to streamline operations, but not all delivering the results I needed. Having been on both sides—first as a user and now as an advisor and product owner—I understand the importance of choosing a system that truly aligns with your business needs. The right ROS can transform your operations, providing you with the insights and control necessary to drive efficiency and profitability. In this section, I'll Walk you through the key factors to consider when choosing an ROS, sharing the lessons I've learned through my journey in the industry. This guide will help you make an informed choice, ensuring that your ROS becomes a powerful ally in your restaurant's success.

Core Functions of a Restaurant Operating System

When selecting a Restaurant Operating System, it's essential to understand the core functions that make it a valuable tool for your business. Through my experience in the industry, I've come to recognize the features that truly matter in an ROS. These systems are not just about automating tasks—they're about integrating every aspect of your restaurant into a cohesive, efficient workflow. A well-chosen ROS should enhance your operations, providing the real-time data and control you need to run a successful restaurant. In this section, I will outline the key functions that any effective ROS should offer, helping you ensure that your choice supports your operational goals and contributes to your bottom line.

An effective ROS should offer comprehensive functionality that covers all areas of restaurant operations. Here are the key functions to consider:

- **Point of Sale (POS)**: Facilitates all types of transactions with efficiency and accuracy.
- **Menu Management**: Supports dynamic menu creation, categorization, pricing, and promotion management.
- **Order Management**: Enhances order processing from creation to tracking, including integration with kitchen display systems.
- **Reservation System**: Manages table assignments, integrates with external booking platforms, and optimizes seating.
- **Staff Management**: Includes scheduling, payroll processing, and shift management functionalities.

- **Customer Relationship Management (CRM):** Maintains customer databases, manages loyalty programs, and gathers customer feedback.

- **Online Ordering and Reservation Systems:** Facilitates online ordering from in-house or third-party platforms and manages online reservations.

- **Billing and Invoicing:** Automates billing, handles multiple payment methods, and supports bill splitting.

- **Integration with Third-Party Services:** Ensures seamless integration with external services like accounting software and food delivery platforms.

- **Compliance and Security:** Guarantees compliance with relevant regulations and secures payment and data transactions.

- **Marketing and Promotions:** Manages promotions and integrates with marketing tools to drive campaigns.

- **Inventory Management:** Provides real-time inventory updates, tracks stock levels, and integrates with POS for accurate management.

- **Reporting and Analytics:** Offers detailed reports and analytics to track sales, inventory, and overall performance.

Vetting the Proper ROS for Your Business

I've seen the difference a well-suited ROS can make. It's not just about finding the most popular or feature-rich system; it's about finding the one that fits your business model, aligns with your operational needs, and scales with your growth. In this section, I'll walk you through the essential factors to consider when vetting a ROS, ensuring you make an informed decision that supports efficiency, accuracy, and profitability in your restaurant.

When choosing an ROS, consider the following factors to ensure it meets your business's unique needs:

1. **Functionality:** Does the ROS have all the features necessary to manage your specific type of restaurant effectively? Ensure it can handle your menu, ordering style, inventory needs, and customer interaction.

2. **Support**: Look for systems that offer reliable customer support. Good support can drastically reduce downtime and improve system reliability.

3. **Cost**: Consider both upfront and ongoing costs. An affordable system that meets your needs can provide a good return on investment. Be wary of systems with hidden fees for updates or additional features.

4. **Hardware Compatibility**: Ensure the ROS works with your existing hardware or that any required hardware is cost-effective and robust.

5. **Ease of Use**: The system should be intuitive and user-friendly. Staff training and adoption will be much smoother with an easy-to-use interface.

6. **Scalability**: Choose an ROS that can grow with your business. It should be flexible enough to accommodate new locations, menu expansions, and increased customer flow.

7. **Integration Capabilities**: The ability to integrate seamlessly with other software and services (like accounting and delivery services) is crucial for maximizing efficiency.

8. **Security Features**: Ensure the system has robust security measures in place to protect sensitive data and comply with payment processing regulations.

By carefully evaluating these aspects, you can choose an ROS that not only meets your current needs but also supports your restaurant's growth and adaptation in a dynamic market environment. The right system will save you time and money, allowing you to focus on delivering exceptional dining experiences.

Part Ten:

Team Roles and Responsibilities

Team Roles and Responsibilities

In my experience leading and building cost control departments across various companies, I've often encountered confusion between the roles of finance and cost control teams. While both are essential for a restaurant's financial health, they serve different functions and require distinct skill sets. Clarifying these roles and responsibilities is crucial for creating a well-functioning team that effectively manages costs and drives profitability.

In this section, I'll share insights from my journey, helping you understand how to structure your teams, define clear roles, and ensure that each department works harmoniously to achieve your restaurant's financial goals.

Cost Controller and Finance

Having established and overseen cost control departments in numerous organizations, I've seen firsthand how critical it is to differentiate between the roles of cost controllers and finance teams. While they often work closely together, their responsibilities are distinct and complementary. The cost controller focuses on managing and analyzing the costs associated with the day-to-day operations, ensuring efficiency and profitability. In contrast, the finance team handles broader financial matters, such as accounting, budgeting, and financial reporting.

Understanding these differences is vital for creating a cohesive strategy that supports both operational excellence and financial stability. In this section, we'll delve into the specific roles and interactions between cost control and finance, ensuring that each plays its part in maintaining the financial health of your restaurant.

Understanding the roles of F&B cost controllers and finance teams, and how they differ in focus and responsibilities.

- **Role Clarity:** Clearly define the roles and responsibilities of the F&B cost controller and finance team. F&B cost controllers focus on managing food and beverage costs, while finance teams oversee overall financial management.

- **Collaboration**: Foster collaboration between F&B cost controller and finance team to ensure comprehensive cost management. Regularly share data and insights to support decision-making.

- **Reporting**: Establish regular reporting mechanisms for the F&B cost controller to provide a detailed cost analysis to the finance team. Use these reports to inform budgeting and financial planning.

- **Training**: Provide training for both roles to understand each other's functions and how they contribute to the overall financial health of the business.

Part Eleven:
Challenges

Challenges

Starting a new restaurant or catering business is an exciting venture, but it comes with its own set of challenges, particularly when it comes to managing costs of goods sold (COGS). Throughout my career, I've encountered and overcome many of these challenges, and I've learned that careful planning and strategic management are key to navigating them successfully.

In this section, I'll share some practical tips and insights that can help you anticipate and address the common hurdles you may face, ensuring your business remains financially healthy from the outset. Whether it's controlling food costs, optimizing inventory, or managing supplier relationships, these strategies will provide you with a solid foundation to tackle the complexities of running a restaurant.

Initial Cost Control

Definition: Initial cost control refers to the strategies and practices implemented at the start of a restaurant or catering business to manage and minimize expenses, particularly the cost of goods sold (COGS).

Introduction: Getting your cost control measures right from the beginning is crucial to the long-term success of your restaurant. In my experience, setting up robust cost control systems at the outset can make the difference between a profitable business and one that struggles to stay afloat. This involves establishing clear procedures for purchasing, inventory management, and pricing. By proactively managing your costs, you can ensure that your business starts on the right foot, avoiding common pitfalls that can eat into your profitability.

In this section, I'll guide you through three key aspects of initial cost control, sharing lessons learned from my own journey in the industry.

Strategies:

- **Budgeting:** Create a detailed budget that includes all startup costs, operational expenses, and contingency funds. Stick to the budget to avoid overspending.

- **Supplier Negotiations:** Establish relationships with suppliers early on. Negotiate favorable terms and bulk discounts to manage costs.

- **Menu Planning:** Develop a menu with a balance of high-margin and popular items. Avoid overly complex dishes that increase COGS.

Managing COGS in a Struggling Businesses

Definition: Managing the Cost of Goods Sold (COGS) in a struggling business involves implementing strategies to reduce expenses and improve profitability, even when a restaurant or catering operation is facing financial difficulties.

Introduction: When a business starts to struggle, managing your COGS becomes more critical than ever. I've worked with several businesses that faced tough times, and I've seen how crucial it is to tighten control over costs to survive. It's not just about cutting expenses but about making smart decisions that can help stabilize the business while still delivering quality to your customers.

In this section, I'll share insights on how to manage COGS effectively in challenging times, drawing from my experiences in turning around businesses facing financial stress. These three strategies can help you navigate through difficult periods and put your business back on the path to profitability.

Strategies:

- **Regular Audits:** Conduct regular audits of inventory, sales, and expenses to identify discrepancies and areas for improvement.

- **Cost Reduction:** Look for opportunities to reduce costs without compromising quality. This could include adjusting portion sizes, finding alternative ingredients, or renegotiating supplier contracts.

- **Waste Management:** Implement strict waste management practices. Train staff on proper storage, handling, and portioning to minimize waste.

Financial Planning

Definition: Financial planning in the context of a restaurant or catering business involves creating detailed budgets and forecasts to manage revenue, expenses, and profitability over a specific period.

Introduction: Financial planning is the backbone of any successful business, especially in the restaurant industry, where margins can be razor-thin. Throughout my career, I've learned that meticulous financial planning is what keeps a business afloat during tough times and propels it forward during good times. Whether you're launching a new venture or trying to steer an existing one through rough waters, having a clear financial plan is essential. In this section, I'll Walk you through two key aspects of financial planning that have proven effective in my own experiences, ensuring you have the tools to forecast accurately, budget wisely, and ultimately secure your business's financial health.

Strategies:

- **Cash Flow Management:** Monitor cash flow closely to ensure there are sufficient funds to cover expenses. Use cash flow forecasts to plan for future needs.

- **Profit Margins:** Regularly review and adjust pricing to maintain healthy profit margins. Ensure that prices reflect changes in ingredient costs.

Part Twelve:

Detailed Case Studies

Detailed Case Studies

The case studies presented in this book are more than just examples; they are reflections of key milestones in my career that have shaped my approach to cost control and restaurant management. Each case study represents a moment when I was faced with a significant challenge that required innovative thinking and decisive action. These were not just problems to solve but opportunities to learn and grow. The solutions I developed not only improved the immediate business situation but also provided me with insights that I carried forward to subsequent roles. These experiences have been invaluable, allowing me to refine strategies, avoid common pitfalls, and make a meaningful impact on the businesses I have been privileged to lead.

In every company I've worked for, these lessons have proven their worth time and again, helping to shift gears and drive the business towards greater efficiency and profitability. The strategies outlined in these case studies have not only solved pressing issues but also laid the groundwork for sustainable success. I hope that by sharing these experiences, other professionals in the industry can benefit from the hard-earned knowledge that has served me so well throughout my career.

Central Kitchen Complexity

Overview

Throughout my career, I've had the privilege of managing and overseeing central kitchens for multiple restaurant outlets, a process that has offered both incredible advantages and significant challenges. Central kitchens are the heartbeat of a restaurant chain, ensuring consistency, efficiency, and cost-effectiveness across various locations. However, I quickly learned that while centralizing production can streamline operations, it also introduces a layer of complexity, particularly when it comes to managing finances and inventory across multiple outlets. These are lessons I've learned firsthand, often through overcoming the very challenges I'm about to share.

Challenges

One of the most persistent challenges I encountered was the issue of double charging costs. It's a subtle yet impactful problem that can easily go unnoticed, especially in the hustle of managing multiple outlets. The crux of the issue lies in how costs are recorded when goods are transferred from the central kitchen to the individual outlets. Both the central kitchen and the outlets tend to log these costs in their general ledger (GL) accounts—once at the point of production and again at the point of sale. This duplication can severely distort the financial picture of each outlet.

Scenario

In one of the central kitchens I managed, we produced large quantities of key ingredients and menu items that were then distributed to various restaurant outlets. The production costs were meticulously recorded in the central kitchen's P&L GL account. However, when these goods were transferred to the outlets, the system would once again log these costs when the items were sold. This resulted in a double counting of costs, inflating the theoretical food cost at the outlet level and causing unnecessary financial strain.

Impact

This duplication led to an inflated food cost at the outlets, making it appear as though they were less profitable than they actually were. It was a frustrating situation that masked the true financial performance of the business and hindered strategic decision-making.

Solutions

1. **System Integration and Configuration:** To tackle this issue, we integrated our POS and inventory management systems, configuring them to distinguish between production costs and transfer costs. This meant that the cost of goods was only logged once—at the central kitchen level—and the outlets' inventory cost basis was adjusted accordingly upon receipt of goods, without duplicating the cost entry.

2. **Inter-branch Transfer Protocols:** We established strict protocols for recording inventory transfers from the central kitchen to the outlets. This included the use of inter-branch transfer receipts that updated inventory levels accurately without affecting cost entries redundantly. It was crucial to ensure that the system recognized these as internal transfers rather than additional purchases.

3. **Periodic Reconciliation:** Regular reconciliations between the central kitchen and the outlets became a staple of our financial processes. This practice helped us catch any discrepancies early on and correct them before they could snowball into larger issues.

4. **Training and Communication:** Recognizing that the success of these systems hinged on the people using them, we invested in thorough training for our financial and inventory management teams. We ensured that everyone, from the central kitchen staff to the outlet managers, understood the unique dynamics of central kitchen operations and how transactions should be recorded.

5. **Advanced Analytics:** Finally, I introduced advanced analytics tools to monitor and analyze the flow of goods and associated costs between the central

kitchen and outlets. This allowed us to spot patterns that could lead to cost discrepancies and make informed decisions to optimize operations further.

Enhancing Strategic Decisions

By addressing these complexities head-on, I was able to ensure accurate financial reporting and leverage the central kitchen's capabilities to make more informed, strategic decisions regarding menu pricing, inventory management, and overall operational efficiency. This experience reinforced the importance of precision and clarity in managing central kitchens, lessons that I've carried forward in every role since.

Multiplication of Articles

Background

Managing inventory in a restaurant is a complex task, and I've seen firsthand how even small oversights can lead to significant issues. One of the challenges I've encountered multiple times is the problem of multiplying similar articles in an inventory system due to inconsistent ingredient branding and purchasing practices. This issue, if not managed properly, can cause serious discrepancies in inventory tracking and food cost calculations—something I learned during my time overseeing operations in a mid-sized casual dining restaurant chain.

Scenario

In this particular restaurant, we relied on a specific brand of milk, Milk Brand A, which was integrated into numerous recipes and registered in our inventory management system. However, due to occasional supply disruptions, our purchasing team would sometimes have to buy an alternative, Milk Brand B. The problem arose because these substitutions were not consistently updated in the system or the recipes.

Challenge

The real issue came to light when Milk Brand A ran out and the kitchen began using Milk Brand B. The system, still tracking Milk Brand A, showed negative inventory levels for it, while Milk Brand B, which was actually being used, remained inaccurately recorded. This inconsistency led to skewed inventory reports, making it difficult to reconcile food costs accurately—a financial headache for any restaurant.

Solution

1. **Unified Ingredient Catalog:** We implemented a policy to standardize ingredient listings in our inventory system. This involved creating a generic entry for ingredients like milk, allowing us to substitute brands without disrupting inventory accuracy or recipe integrity.

2. **System Training and Updates:** Recognizing that this was also a human issue, we conducted training sessions for our purchasing and kitchen staff, emphasizing

the importance of updating the inventory system whenever substitutions occurred. We also upgraded our inventory management software to support more flexible ingredient substitutions, ensuring that these changes were automatically reflected in the system.

3. **Regular Inventory Audits:** We introduced more frequent physical inventory checks. This allowed us to catch discrepancies quickly, ensuring that our system data always matched actual stock levels.

4. **Vendor Communication and Management:** Strengthening our communication with suppliers was key. We set up alerts to notify us when key ingredients were running low, allowing us to reorder in a timely manner and avoid last-minute substitutions.

Outcome

These solutions drastically reduced inventory discrepancies in the restaurant. The unified ingredient catalog allowed us to substitute ingredients as needed without affecting the accuracy of our inventory. Training and system updates ensured that any substitutions were immediately reflected, and regular audits helped maintain accurate tracking.

Financial Impact

By resolving these inventory issues, we achieved much more accurate food cost calculations. With correct inventory levels, we could forecast costs better and reduce waste. This improved inventory management also strengthened our position during supplier negotiations, leading to more favorable terms and better pricing, which had a positive impact on the restaurant's overall profitability.

Lessons Learned

This experience reinforced the importance of a flexible yet rigorous inventory management system in the restaurant industry. Accurate records and the ability to adapt to supply variations without compromising data integrity are crucial for effective food cost management and overall financial health. This is a lesson I've carried forward into every subsequent role, helping to optimize operations and drive profitability in each of the businesses I've managed.

Price Locking in Inventory Control

Background

Throughout my career, I've learned that even the best-laid plans can go awry if the right systems and checks aren't in place. One such critical system is price locking within inventory management. This is a feature that I've championed across the businesses I've managed, and its importance was underscored by a particular incident that could have led to a significant financial loss.

Situation

In one of the bustling seafood restaurants I managed, we had a standing agreement with a supplier for fresh whole tuna at $8 per kilogram. This supplier relationship had been built on trust and consistency, but one day, our Chef de Partie (CDP) received a shipment and, in the rush of the day, signed the Goods Received Note (GRN) without verifying the price—something that usually wouldn't have been an issue.

Complication

However, when the CDP tried to enter the received goods into our inventory system, an error message popped up. The system had detected a price discrepancy—the invoice listed the tuna at $25 per kilogram, a staggering increase from our agreed-upon price. Upon investigation, we discovered that the supplier had mistakenly sent sashimi-grade Tuna Loins from Southeast Asia instead of the whole tuna we typically ordered.

Resolution

Thankfully, our inventory management system had a price locking feature enabled. This technology flagged the error immediately, preventing the entry of the inflated price into our system. The CDP was able to catch the mistake before it affected our inventory records or, worse, our food cost percentages. A quick call to the supplier resolved the issue—they promptly replaced the shipment with the correct grade of tuna at the agreed price.

Outcome

By catching the error early, we avoided what would have been a dramatic increase in food costs for dishes featuring tuna, protecting our margins and ensuring that our pricing strategy remained intact. This incident reaffirmed the importance of stringent controls and protocols in restaurant operations.

Lessons Learned

- **Price Verification:** Even with advanced systems in place, it's crucial to manually verify prices upon receipt of goods to ensure no discrepancies slip through.

- **Supplier Communication:** Clear and continuous communication with suppliers is essential to avoid costly mistakes like this one.

- **Staff Training:** Training staff on the importance of checking prices and understanding the protocols for handling discrepancies is vital to maintaining control over food costs.

Conclusion

This experience illustrates the critical role that technological safeguards, like price locking, play in maintaining control over food costs. It's a feature I've insisted on in every restaurant I've managed, knowing that it can protect against the kind of costly errors that can erode profitability. Integrating such systems into your operations isn't just a luxury; it's a necessity for safeguarding your business's financial health.

Effective Portion Control

Background

During my time managing a popular casual dining restaurant, I encountered a significant issue that many restaurant operators face: inconsistencies in portion sizes. We prided ourselves on delivering high-quality dishes, but I began noticing that customer complaints about portion sizes were on the rise. Not only were these inconsistencies affecting our guests' dining experiences, but they were also leading to fluctuating food costs, which made it difficult to maintain our desired profit margins. I realized that we needed to address this issue head-on to uphold our standards and ensure the sustainability of the business.

Objective

My goal was clear: to implement a reliable system for portion control that would enhance customer satisfaction and bring stability to our food costs. I wanted to create a kitchen environment where every dish that left the pass was consistent in both quality and quantity, ensuring that our guests knew exactly what to expect every time they dined with us.

Implementation

Assessment and Training: Drawing from my years of experience in the industry, I knew that the first step was to thoroughly assess our current operations. It became evident that our kitchen lacked standardized procedures for portioning, leading to significant variations in dish sizes. I personally led training sessions with our kitchen staff, emphasizing the importance of portion control—not just for cost management but as a cornerstone of our commitment to quality.

Standardization of Recipes: Leveraging my expertise, I worked closely with our chefs to standardize our recipes. We meticulously documented each one, specifying precise ingredient measurements and creating detailed portion control charts. I made sure that these standards were not just written down but were clearly communicated to every member of the kitchen team.

Implementation of Tools: To support the new standards, I introduced specialized kitchen tools such as scales, portion scoops, and measuring cups at every station. I conducted hands-on demonstrations to ensure that the staff were comfortable and proficient with these tools. It was essential to me that these tools became an integral part of our daily operations.

Routine Monitoring: I implemented a routine monitoring system where I, along with my senior kitchen staff, would conduct regular checks to ensure compliance with the new portion control measures. I believed that ongoing oversight was crucial to maintaining the discipline needed for consistent portioning.

Feedback Loop: Understanding the importance of continuous improvement, I established a feedback loop involving both our customers and staff. We actively sought customer feedback on portion sizes and invited kitchen staff to share their experiences and challenges with the new system. This approach not only kept everyone engaged but also allowed us to make real-time adjustments to our processes.

Results

Consistency in Meal Quality: The results were remarkable. We quickly saw a significant improvement in the consistency of our dishes. Guests appreciated the uniformity and positive feedback became more frequent. This consistency became a hallmark of our restaurant, setting us apart from competitors.

Stabilized Food Costs: With the portion control measures firmly in place, our food costs stabilized. By reducing waste and ensuring accurate ingredient usage, we were able to forecast food costs more precisely, which significantly improved our profitability.

Reduced Waste: The introduction of portion control tools and standardized recipes led to a notable reduction in food waste. This not only had a positive impact on our bottom line but also aligned with my commitment to sustainable practices within the restaurant.

Lessons Learned

This experience reinforced a fundamental lesson for me: effective portion control is indispensable in the restaurant industry. The success we achieved through these measures was a direct result of the rigorous standards we implemented and the dedication of our team to uphold them. This approach to portion control became a blueprint that I carried with me into future projects, consistently applying these principles to drive quality, customer satisfaction, and profitability. For anyone managing a restaurant, I can confidently say that investing time and effort into proper portion control is one of the most impactful strategies you can adopt.

Vendor Negotiation and Supply Chain Management

Background

During my time managing a restaurant, I encountered a common yet challenging situation: rising ingredient costs were starting to eat into our profitability. The restaurant had long relied on a single-source supplier strategy, which, while convenient, had led to complacency on both sides. With no competition, our supplier had little incentive to keep prices competitive, and we were feeling the impact on our bottom line. As someone who's always believed in the power of strategic vendor relationships, I knew it was time to shake things up.

Objective

My primary objective was to reduce our ingredient costs without compromising on quality. At the same time, I wanted to build a more resilient supply chain that could withstand disruptions, something particularly important for a family-run business with a limited financial buffer. The goal was not just about saving money in the short term but ensuring long-term sustainability and profitability.

Implementation

Engaging Multiple Vendors: The first step was to move away from the reliance on a single supplier. I began reaching out to multiple vendors for our key ingredients—everything from olive oil to pasta and tomatoes. By bringing in more players, I aimed to introduce competition into our supply chain, which I believed would naturally drive prices down.

Competitive Bidding Process: I initiated a competitive bidding process, where each vendor had the opportunity to provide quotes for the same set of products. This process was transparent and allowed us to compare not just prices but also the quality of the ingredients and the terms offered. It was crucial to maintain the high standards our customers expected, so quality remained a top priority.

Negotiating Prices and Terms: Armed with quotes from multiple vendors, I began negotiating. This was where my experience really came into play. I wasn't just looking for the lowest price; I wanted the best overall deal, which included favorable payment terms, reliable delivery schedules, and the flexibility to scale up or down based on demand. By playing vendors against each other, I was able to secure better pricing and more favorable terms.

Building Resilience: In addition to securing better deals, I focused on building a more resilient supply chain. I ensured that we had at least two suppliers for every key ingredient, which reduced our dependency on any single source. This approach not only lowered costs but also mitigated the risk of supply disruptions, whether due to unforeseen events or issues within a particular supplier's operations.

Training and Implementation: Once the new vendor relationships were established, I worked closely with our purchasing team to implement the changes. It was important that everyone understood the new processes, including how to handle orders, manage inventory from multiple sources, and maintain the quality standards we were known for.

Results

Lowered Ingredient Costs: Through strategic vendor negotiation and the introduction of competition, we successfully reduced our ingredient costs by 15%. This was a significant saving, directly contributing to an improved profit margin for the restaurant.

Improved Supply Chain Resilience: By diversifying our supplier base, we greatly reduced the risk of supply chain disruptions. This meant that even if one supplier faced issues, we had alternatives in place to ensure continuity of service, which is critical in the restaurant business.

Enhanced Financial Health: The cost savings, coupled with a more resilient supply chain, led to a noticeable improvement in the restaurant's financial health. This strengthened our position in the market and provided a solid foundation for future growth.

Lessons Learned

This experience reinforced the importance of proactive vendor management in the restaurant industry. Relying on a single supplier can be convenient, but it often leads to complacency and higher costs. By introducing competition, negotiating strategically, and building a resilient supply chain, you can significantly enhance your business's financial performance and operational stability. This approach has since become a cornerstone of my strategy in every restaurant I manage, and I strongly recommend it to anyone looking to optimize their supply chain and improve profitability.

Dynamic Pricing Strategy

Background

I was brought in as a consultant by a seafood restaurant located in a bustling coastal area that was grappling with fluctuating seafood prices. The unpredictability of seafood costs, influenced by factors such as seasonal availability, weather conditions, and market demand, was causing significant swings in the restaurant's food cost percentages. This volatility not only threatened profitability but also posed challenges in maintaining consistent pricing for customers.

Objective

The primary objective of my consultancy work was to help the restaurant maintain stable profit margins despite the fluctuating cost of seafood. Additionally, we aimed to increase transparency with customers regarding the reasons behind price changes, ultimately fostering trust and loyalty. The goal was to develop a pricing model that could adapt to market changes without compromising on profitability or customer satisfaction.

Implementation

Market Research: I began by conducting thorough market research to understand the factors influencing seafood prices. This involved closely monitoring trends, including seasonal variations and supply chain issues, that impacted seafood availability and costs. These insights were crucial in formulating a responsive pricing strategy.

Developing a Dynamic Pricing Model: Based on the research, I helped the restaurant implement a dynamic pricing strategy. This model allowed the restaurant to adjust menu prices in real-time or on a daily basis, depending on the market cost of seafood. For example, the price of popular dishes like lobster or oysters could fluctuate based on the day's market rate, ensuring that the restaurant's food cost percentage remained within target margins.

Customer Communication: Transparency was key to the success of this strategy. We introduced clear communication strategies about the dynamic pricing model, including notes on the menus explaining that seafood prices were subject to change based on market conditions. Additionally, I trained the staff to effectively communicate this pricing strategy to customers, emphasizing the freshness and quality of the seafood as a justification for any price fluctuations.

POS System Integration: I recommended updates to the restaurant's point-of-sale (POS) system to accommodate the dynamic pricing model. This integration allowed for seamless adjustments to menu prices, ensuring that the pricing reflected the current market conditions in real time. The use of technology made it easier for the management to update prices across all platforms, from digital menus to printed copies.

Monitoring and Adjusting: Throughout the consultancy, I continuously monitored the effectiveness of the dynamic pricing strategy. We tracked customer reactions, sales data, and profit margins to ensure that the strategy was achieving the desired outcomes. Based on this data, we made adjustments to the pricing model as necessary, refining the approach over time.

Results

Maintained Profit Margins: The dynamic pricing strategy successfully protected the restaurant's profit margins, even during periods of significant cost increases. By adjusting menu prices in line with market costs, the restaurant avoided the financial strain that typically accompanies fluctuating ingredient prices.

Increased Transparency and Trust: Customers appreciated the transparency provided by the restaurant regarding its pricing strategy. By clearly communicating the reasons for price changes, the restaurant built trust with its patrons, which in turn increased customer loyalty. Regular guests understood that they were paying for quality and freshness, which justified the variable pricing.

Improved Customer Loyalty: The restaurant saw an increase in customer loyalty, as patrons valued the honesty and quality of the dining experience. The transparency around pricing not only mitigated potential frustration but also positioned the restaurant as a trustworthy and customer-focused establishment.

Lessons Learned

This consultancy project highlights the importance of flexibility and transparency in pricing strategies, particularly in industries prone to cost fluctuations. By implementing a dynamic pricing model, the restaurant was able to safeguard its profit margins while maintaining customer trust and loyalty. The key takeaway is that customers are willing to accept variable pricing if they understand the reasons behind it and perceive value in the product being offered. This approach can be particularly effective for restaurants dealing with volatile ingredient costs, ensuring financial stability without compromising customer relationships.

Leveraging Inventory & Capacity

Background

At one of the casual dining restaurants I managed, we faced the dual challenge of seasonal fluctuations and the growing demand for delivery services. With a diverse menu and a well-stocked kitchen, I saw an opportunity to maximize our resources by creating a ghost kitchen brand that would operate exclusively online, focusing on a sandwich menu.

Objective

The goal was straightforward: boost revenue without significantly increasing costs. By utilizing ingredients we already had on hand, we aimed to develop a secondary menu that could be offered under a new brand, specifically targeting the online delivery market. This approach was designed to help mitigate the impact of the slow season while reaching a new customer segment.

Implementation

Menu Development: We started by developing a sandwich menu that utilized the same ingredients from our main menu. This was crucial in ensuring we didn't disrupt our existing inventory processes or require additional storage space.

Brand Creation: A fresh brand identity was crafted for the ghost kitchen, appealing to the online delivery market. This brand was launched exclusively on popular food delivery platforms, allowing us to tap into the growing demand for at-home dining.

Operational Adjustments: Our kitchen staff received training to prepare both the main restaurant's dishes and the new ghost kitchen sandwiches. This dual use of labor and kitchen space was key to maintaining operational efficiency.

Marketing Strategy: Targeted online marketing campaigns, including social media ads and partnerships with delivery apps, were rolled out to introduce and promote the ghost kitchen brand to potential customers.

Technology Integration: We upgraded our POS system to manage orders for both the main and ghost kitchen menus seamlessly. This integration allowed for accurate inventory tracking and streamlined order management across both brands.

Results

Increased Revenue: The ghost kitchen successfully generated additional income, providing a financial boost during the slower season.

Optimized Inventory Usage: By sharing ingredients across both brands, we minimized waste and maximized inventory efficiency.

Enhanced Operational Efficiency: The shared use of kitchen space and labor resulted in lower production costs per unit, improving overall operational efficiency.

Expanded Market Reach: The online-only brand attracted a different customer base from our dine-in clientele, diversifying our revenue streams.

Lessons Learned

This experience reinforced the power of innovation and flexibility in the restaurant industry. By leveraging existing resources and adapting to market trends, we were able to create a new revenue stream with minimal additional investment. This approach not only sustained the business during a slow season but also opened up new avenues for growth. It's a strategy I've carried forward in my career, always looking for ways to maximize efficiency and explore new opportunities within the constraints of existing resources.

Menu Optimization for Cost Efficiency

Background

I managed an upscale restaurant that had no shortage of customers; the dining room was always full, and reservations were hard to come by. However, despite this high traffic, I noticed that our profitability was not where it should be. It was a frustrating paradox: a bustling restaurant with underwhelming financial returns. I knew we needed to dig deeper to find the root cause, and I suspected that the menu was where we needed to focus our attention.

Objective

The primary goal was to increase profitability without sacrificing the quality and appeal that our restaurant was known for. I aimed to identify which menu items were dragging down our profits and find ways to either improve their margins or phase them out in favor of more profitable alternatives. This was not just about trimming the fat—it was about refining our offerings to better align with both our brand and our financial goals.

Implementation

Comprehensive Menu Analysis: Drawing on my experience in menu engineering, I initiated a thorough analysis of our existing menu. I looked at each dish, examining its food cost percentage, popularity, and overall contribution to the restaurant's profitability. It quickly became evident that several high-cost, low-margin items were skewing our profitability, even though they were popular with customers.

Revising Menu Offerings: Armed with this data, I began the process of revising the menu. I worked closely with our chefs to either eliminate the low-margin items or redesign them using more cost-effective ingredients. The challenge was to maintain the high standards our customers expected while reducing costs. For some dishes, this meant finding alternative suppliers or tweaking recipes to achieve better margins without compromising taste or presentation.

A Focus on High-Margin Items: We also identified dishes that were both popular and profitable. I made these the focal point of our new menu, giving them prominent placement and even creating special promotions around them. This strategic shift not only helped streamline kitchen operations by focusing on fewer, more profitable dishes but also resonated well with our customers.

Redesigning Recipes: For those dishes that had potential but were not performing financially, I worked with the culinary team to redesign the recipes. We found ways to substitute expensive ingredients with more affordable ones or adjusted portion sizes slightly to improve margins. Throughout this process, I was meticulous in ensuring that the quality and flavor of our dishes remained top-notch—after all, our reputation depended on it.

Training and Relaunch: Once the new menu was finalized, I conducted training sessions with the kitchen and service staff. It was crucial that everyone understood the importance of the changes and how to communicate them effectively to our guests. We also used this opportunity to relaunch the menu with a bit of fanfare, highlighting the new items and improved offerings to our regular customers.

Results

Increased Profitability: The impact of these changes was immediate and measurable. Our food cost percentage improved significantly, and the restaurant's profitability saw a noticeable uptick. The streamlined menu allowed us to focus on dishes that not only delighted our customers but also supported our financial goals.

Streamlined Kitchen Operation: With a more focused menu, kitchen operations became more efficient. The reduced complexity in our offerings meant that the kitchen could operate more smoothly, with fewer bottlenecks during peak times. This efficiency also contributed to lower labor costs and reduced waste.

Enhanced Menu Appeal: Far from alienating our customers, the menu revisions enhanced our restaurant's appeal. The new offerings were well-received, and the focus on quality, high-margin dishes reinforced our brand's reputation for excellence. Customers appreciated the refined choices, and the positive feedback rolled in.

Lessons Learned

This experience underscored the importance of regular menu evaluation as a key strategy for maintaining profitability in the restaurant industry. It's not enough to have a menu that brings in customers; it must also bring in profits. Through careful analysis and thoughtful revisions, we were able to transform our menu into a powerful tool for financial success. This approach to menu optimization has since become a cornerstone of my work, and I continue to advocate for its importance in every restaurant I manage or consult. For anyone in the industry, I can't stress enough how critical it is to regularly reassess your menu and ensure that it aligns with both your culinary vision and your financial objectives.

Training and Monitoring for Theft Prevention

Background

In a high-volume quick-service restaurant (QSR) that I managed, persistent discrepancies in food and packaging costs began to raise red flags. These discrepancies suggested possible internal theft, a critical issue that needed to be addressed immediately to protect the restaurant's profitability and ensure operational integrity.

Scenario

The restaurant was experiencing unexplained variances in inventory, particularly in food and packaging items. Given the high turnover and fast pace of operations, these discrepancies were initially hard to track, but they pointed towards potential internal theft—a challenge that, if left unchecked, could lead to significant financial losses.

Challenge

The key challenge was not just identifying the source of the discrepancies but also implementing measures that would prevent future occurrences. With multiple staff members handling inventory and packaging, there was a need for a robust system that could provide accountability and transparency across all levels of operation.

Implementation

Enhanced Surveillance System: We upgraded our surveillance systems to cover more areas within the restaurant, ensuring that all inventory movement was monitored closely.

Stringent Inventory Check: Introduced more frequent and detailed inventory audits, with a particular focus on high-risk items. These checks were designed to quickly identify any discrepancies between recorded and actual stock levels.

Staff Training on Accountability: Conducted targeted training sessions to educate staff about the importance of accountability and the ethical implications of theft. This training emphasized the consequences of inventory theft, both for the individual and the business.

Packaging Management Integration: Integrated packaging costs into our recipe costing, segregating between takeaway and dine-in options. This allowed us to track packaging use more accurately and link it directly to sales data.

Monitoring Discrepancies: Implemented a system to monitor discrepancies between packaging inventory and sales, enabling us to quickly identify and address any irregularities.

Results

These measures led to a significant reduction in cost discrepancies, restoring accuracy to our inventory records. The improved internal controls not only curbed potential theft but also reinforced a culture of honesty and accountability within the team. By taking these steps, we were able to protect the restaurant's financial health and maintain trust among staff, ultimately contributing to a more secure and efficient operation.

Lessons Learned

Proactive Measures Are Essential: Addressing potential theft before it escalates is crucial. Implementing proactive measures like enhanced surveillance and frequent inventory checks can prevent significant losses and maintain the integrity of the business.

Staff Training is Important: Regular training sessions on accountability and ethics are vital in fostering a culture of honesty. Educating staff about the impact of theft on the business and their roles in maintaining inventory accuracy is key to preventing internal theft.

Integration of Packaging Cost: Including packaging in the recipe costing process and segregating it between dine-in and takeaway options provides a more accurate picture of overall costs. This integration helps in identifying discrepancies more efficiently.

Continuous Monitoring and Auditing: Regular monitoring of inventory against sales and implementing thorough audits are necessary to maintain control over stock levels. This ensures that any discrepancies are identified and resolved promptly.

Building a Culture of Accountability: Creating a work environment where staff feel responsible for their actions and understand the consequences of theft leads to a more secure and trustworthy operation. Encouraging transparency and accountability can significantly reduce the risk of internal theft.

Inventory Management in a Multi-Stage Production Process

Scenario

As one of the leaders in a company that roasts and sells its own coffee, we faced significant challenges in accurately costing our coffee beans and managing inventory across various stages of production. The initially implemented process was based on a weighted average cost approach for all coffees, given that we import around twenty-four different types of beans, some sold as single origin and others as blends. However, this approach was flawed and led to numerous issues, including:

- Inaccurate costing per type of bean.

- Inability to monitor coffee consumption by quantity or specific beans.

- Lack of insight into which coffee beans were more popular.

- Difficulty generating trend reports from the system.

- Poor control over theft prevention and losses.

- Frequent discrepancies in inventory management.

Solution

To address these challenges, we restructured our inventory and costing processes to reflect the complexity of our operations, ensuring accuracy and control at each stage:

Receiving and Initial Storage: We began by registering the green coffee beans upon receipt into a specific inventory location, labeled as the *Green Beans Warehouse (W/H)*. This ensured that all incoming beans were tracked from the moment they entered our facility.

Stage Costing from Green to Roasted Beans: The beans were then moved through a stage costing process as they transitioned from green to roasted beans. At this stage, the roasted beans were transferred to a separate location called the *Roasted Beans Warehouse (W/H)*. This allowed us to track the costs associated with roasting and ensured that each type of bean retained its specific cost.

Packaging and Final Preparation: Once roasted, the beans were packaged in various sizes and formats—whether as blends, single origins, or specific retail products. These were then categorized as either semi-finished or finished goods, depending on whether they were ready for sale or needed further processing. These items were stored in their respective inventory locations, accurately reflecting their stage in the production process.

Sales Channels and Inventory Depletion: Packaged beans were sold through multiple channels, including retail, ecommerce, and wholesale. The system was set up to deplete inventory based on the specific type of bean sold, ensuring accurate tracking of stock levels and sales.

Café Operations and POS Integration: For our café operations, coffee moved to another stage of production, where it was prepared and sold as beverages. We implemented two methods for registering customer orders at the point of sale (POS):

- **Direct Button:** For pure coffee orders, where the customer selects a specific type of bean.

- **Modifier Button:** For mixed coffee beverages, such as lattes or cappuccinos, where the customer could choose their preferred bean. This approach allowed us to accurately reflect the cost and consumption of each bean, ensuring precise inventory depletion and sales reporting.

Outcome

Improved Cost Accuracy: By tracking each stage of production and accurately costing each type of bean, we were able to generate precise reports and control costs effectively.

Enhanced Inventory Control: We gained visibility into which beans were more popular, allowing us to optimize inventory levels and reduce waste.

Better Theft and Loss Prevention: The detailed tracking at each stage helped us identify and prevent theft and losses.

Data-Driven Insights: The system now provides valuable insights into sales trends and customer preferences, enabling more informed business decisions.

Lessons Learned

This case study underscores the importance of detailed and accurate inventory management in a multi-stage production process. By moving away from a generalized costing approach and implementing stage-specific tracking and costing, we were able to gain control over our operations, improve profitability, and make data-driven decisions that aligned with our business goals. This experience has been invaluable in refining our approach to inventory management and ensuring that every bean is accounted for, from farm to cup.

Managing Complexity in Airline Catering Operations

Background

Airline catering is a behemoth of an operation, especially when you're responsible for preparing over two hundred thousand meals per day. The sheer volume, coupled with the need for precision and consistency, makes it one of the most complex food production environments. In my career, I've had the opportunity to delve into this complexity, understanding the intricacies involved in breaking down such a massive operation into manageable, cost-effective stages. This case study explores how leveraging AI and systematic planning can help manage the complexity and ensure accurate costing and inventory control.

Objective

The primary objective is to implement a comprehensive system that can manage the diverse and voluminous needs of airline catering. This includes ensuring accurate costing, efficient inventory management, and timely production while maintaining the highest standards of food safety and quality. The system must be capable of handling the multitude of variables involved, from daily menu changes to special dietary requirements and preparing meals months in advance for optimal readiness.

Challenges

Menu Diversity:

- **Daily Course Variation:** Breakfast, lunch, snacks, and dinner menus vary daily.

- **Destination-Specific Menus:** Different menus are required for various routes, considering the origin and destination, resulting in hundreds of different dishes that rotate quarterly.

- **Special Meals:** The need to cater to diverse dietary requirements (e.g., gluten-free, vegan, low-calorie) adds another layer of complexity, with at least a dozen variations to manage.

Long-Term Planning:

- Meals must be prepared and frozen months ahead of time to ensure availability and longevity, and to avoid complicating the inventory and production scheduling.

Ingredient Sourcing:

- The vast number of ingredients required for such a diverse menu presents challenges in procurement, storage, and quality control, with the need to source, store, and manage these ingredients effectively.

Tracking Movements and Capturing Costs:

- The complexity of tracking all inventory movements—from sourcing, production, and freezing to final delivery—while accurately capturing the associated costs is a significant challenge. Each stage of production involves multiple transitions that must be carefully monitored to ensure that costs are allocated correctly, and that no discrepancies arise that could affect the overall financial accuracy of the operation.

Solution

Stage-by-Stage Breakdown:

- **Siloed Production Stages:** The operation is broken down into silos, each responsible for a specific aspect of the meal preparation process. These include:
- **Ingredient Sourcing:** Centralized procurement teams manage the supply chain for all necessary ingredients, ensuring consistent quality and availability.
- **Batch Preparation:** Large-scale batch preparation of core ingredients and components, categorized by meal type (e.g., breakfast components, sauces for dinner).
- **Special Meal Preparation:** Dedicated silos for preparing and packaging special meals, ensuring compliance with dietary requirements.
- **Freezing and Storage:** Once prepared, meals are flash-frozen and stored in a centralized facility, with inventory tracked meticulously to ensure freshness and

availability.

AI Integration:

- **Pre-approved Recipes:** AI systems are employed to generate pre-approved recipes, adjusting them dynamically based on ingredient availability, cost fluctuations, and seasonal variations.

- **Demand Forecasting:** AI-driven forecasting tools predict the number of meals required for each route and menu variation, allowing for precise production planning.

- **Inventory Management:** AI monitors inventory levels in real-time, optimizing the flow of ingredients through the various silos and ensuring that stock levels are maintained without overproduction.

Comprehensive Costing System:

- **Granular Cost Tracking:** Each stage of the production process is costed separately, with expenses tracked at every step. This ensures that the overall cost of each meal is accurately calculated, accounting for variations in ingredient costs, labor, and overhead.

- **Unified System Integration:** All silos feed into a centralized system, which consolidates the data to provide a clear, overarching view of the operation. This system handles the complexities of calculating the cost per meal, managing inventory across stages, and tracking the financial impact of each decision.

- **Continuous Feedback Loops:** Regular reviews and adjustments are made based on the data collected, ensuring that the system remains responsive to changes in demand, supply, and cost structures.

Results

Freezing and Storage: Once prepared, meals are flash-frozen and stored in a centralized facility, with inventory tracked meticulously to ensure freshness and availability.

Accurate Costing: The detailed breakdown and use of AI allowed for precise costing of each meal, with clear visibility into the cost drivers at each stage of production.

Inventory Control: Improved inventory management, reduced waste and ensured that all necessary ingredients were available when needed, minimizing the risk of stockouts or overstocking.

Operational Efficiency: The system's ability to forecast demand accurately and adjust production accordingly led to significant improvements in operational efficiency, reducing both labor and material costs.

Enhanced Flexibility: The operation could adapt to changing circumstances quickly, whether due to shifts in demand, ingredient availability, or cost changes, thanks to the integrated system and AI tools.

Lessons Learned

This case study underscores the importance of breaking down complex operations into manageable stages, each with its own set of controls and cost-tracking mechanisms. By integrating AI and a centralized system, the airline catering operation was able to maintain high standards of quality and efficiency, despite the overwhelming complexity. This approach can be applied to other large-scale food production environments, demonstrating the value of advanced technology and meticulous planning in modern food service operations.

Conclusion

Congratulations on completing "The Food Cost Mastery." As we wrap up this comprehensive exploration of effective food cost management, remember that the journey to mastery is continuous. The strategies and techniques discussed are not just theories but practical tools to be woven into the daily fabric of your restaurant operations for better efficiency, profitability, and sustainability.

At the core of successful cost control is a deep understanding of your costs, meticulous inventory management, and strategic pricing. These elements require making informed decisions based on robust data, continuously monitoring financial performance, and proactively addressing challenges as they arise.

The restaurant industry is ever-evolving, demanding innovation and flexibility to stay competitive. Apply the insights from "The Food Cost Mastery" to adapt to market trends, refine your strategies, and ensure your business remains ahead of the curve. Whether optimizing your menu, employing demand-based pricing, or enhancing inventory procedures, each incremental improvement can significantly boost your bottom line.

This book aims to arm you with the knowledge to not just survive but thrive in the competitive restaurant landscape. Keep learning, experimenting, and refining your approach to meet and exceed your financial objectives. Thank you for choosing "The Food Cost Mastery" as your guide. Here's to your continued success in the world of culinary business!

Acknowledgments

I am profoundly grateful to the esteemed faculty at the Blue Mountains International Hotel Management School. Each professor played a pivotal role in shaping my understanding and passion for the hospitality industry. Their dedication to imparting deep academic knowledge and practical insights has been invaluable to my professional growth. This book is a reflection of the rigorous training and comprehensive education I received under their guidance, and I am deeply thankful for their unwavering support and expertise.

In addition to my academic foundation, I owe a great deal of my professional growth to the diverse experiences I've had in the industry. I want to express my deep gratitude to the companies I have worked for and to the managers who played pivotal roles in my journey. To those who recognized my potential, provided me with the space to innovate, and trusted my abilities—I thank you for your mentorship and the opportunities you gave me to excel. Your support allowed me to push boundaries and achieve more than I could have imagined.

I am also thankful for the challenging experiences with difficult managers, even those whose actions were less than supportive. These experiences, though tough, taught me resilience and the importance of maintaining my ethics and integrity, no matter the circumstances. These trials pushed me to develop not just professionally but personally, and ultimately strengthened my resolve to contribute positively to the industry.

To all those who have been a part of my journey—whether as allies or adversaries—I acknowledge your impact on my career. Every experience, both good and bad, has shaped my path and fueled my passion for excellence in the hospitality industry.

About The Author

Wissam Baghdadi's journey from the war-torn streets of Beirut to the heights of the global hospitality and tech industries encapsulates a remarkable story of resilience and ambition. Born in Beirut in 1978, Wissam moved to Australia in 1998 to pursue a degree in International Hospitality and Tourism Management at the BMIHMS. Starting as a dishwasher while studying, he quickly climbed the ranks of the hospitality world. His extensive career includes time with Emirates Airlines and a venture into entrepreneurship with his own restaurant in Algeria. Wissam significantly shaped the F&B landscape during his twelve-year tenure at Del Monte Fresh Produce, where he created a QSR concept and launched -five locations across the Middle East and North America. He also founded Restauratomy in the US, offering tailored consultancy services to the restaurant industry.

Now, as the COO of Caffeine Lab, he drives growth in the coffee industry. Concurrently, Wissam contributes his vast expertise to Jalebi.io as an advisor and product owner, pioneering sophisticated Restaurant Operating Systems to enhance F&B operations globally.

Through his book, "The Food Cost Mastery," Wissam aims to impart his comprehensive knowledge to restaurateurs seeking to refine their operations and achieve peak profitability.

www.ingramcontent.com/pod-product-compliance
Lightning Source LLC
Chambersburg PA
CBHW052342210326
41597CB00037B/6222